Praise for LOU BRUTUS

"I value Lou for bringing an unrivaled integrity to the world of Hard Rock reporting. His honest discussions are straight from the heart on both sides of the mic. He makes artists and fans worlds' collide in the best possible way."

—ZACKY VENGEANCE, of Avenged Sevenfold

"There's nothing more inspiring than a person in love with what they're doing. When you run in to Lou at a festival he has that look of amazement in his eyes as if he just heard an electric guitar for the first time and he just has to let the world know. That passion and love for the music and the stories waiting to be told is what makes him such a master of his craft."

—JOHANNES ECKERSTRÖM, of Avatar

"Who is this Lou Brutus? We've gotten to know each other over the years, very well. Lou is a mainstay of rock and roll. He's a pioneer, and a legend. To top it off he's one hell of a human being. He cares about people, and people care about him. A lot. Lou is someone I always look forward to seeing. I look forward to having conversations with him. Meaningful conversations. He's brilliant and he's got so many great stories to tell. Here's to Lou Brutus!"

—ADAM GONTIER, of Saint Asonia

"There are musicians that make the music, there are fans looking to feed their never-ending hunger for great music, and then there is that 'Conduit' in the middle. That person with a résumé of integrity in "knowing" music—a bigger-than-life voice! A tastemaker that earns the respect, trust, and friendship of both musicians and music fans alike. A voice that turns the fans onto great music and helps to turn those musicians into rock stars. Lou Brutus is that conduit and more! Giving intelligent interviews, curating incredible radio playlists, identifying 'the next big thing' in new music, capturing rock moments in time, master of ceremonies at major concerts, and last but not least, singing in his own punk band. Lou Brutus LIVES MUSIC! Lou Brutus is ROCK!""

—JESSE JAMES DUPREE, of Jackyl

"Lou Brutus is the most genuine radio guy in the biz. He's gone above and beyond for us since the day we met. A class act and a true to the bone music fan as well."

—ALECIA MIXI DEMNER, of Stitched Up Heart

"It is an objective reality that rock no longer has the same share of the mainstream limelight that it once had. As a result, it seems that many voices have distanced themselves from the genre. Lou, however, has only dug in more. Furthermore, Lou actively seeks bands out and makes his own assessments. This continued passion and fandom is a testament to Lou's love for the genre—especially when you consider that he has rubbed elbows and befriended so many of the greatest. His ability to have an engaged and nuanced interest in the newest crop of bands while being fully enmeshed with the biggest bands out there solidifies his position as a true tastemaker and the narrator of rock. In short, he is a treasure to the genre."

—DUSTIN BATES, of Starset

"Lou Brutus has got to be the most knowledgeable, die-hard music fan I've ever met. Always supporting bands of all genres. I've been lucky enough to have known him my entire twenty-two year career. He's flown the flag for my band, as well as so many others, throughout his career in the music industry. Whether it's doing an interview with him (which are always the best), or just talking baseball, he's always been my favorite person to talk too. My dear friend, Lou. I love you, buddy."

—MORGAN ROSE, of Sevendust

SONIC WARRIOR

LOU BRUTUS
SONIC WARRIOR
MY LIFE AS A ROCK N ROLL REPROBATE
(TALES OF SEX, DRUGS, AND VOMITING AT INOPPORTUNE MOMENTS)

FOREWORD BY COREY TAYLOR
ILLUSTRATIONS BY ALAN MACBAIN

RARE BIRD BOOKS
LOS ANGELES, CALIF.

Set in Warnock
Printed in the United States

10 9 8 7 6 5 4 3 2 1

Library of Congress Cataloging-in-Publication Data

Names: Brutus, Lou, 1962– author.
Title: Sonic Warrior My Life as a Rock and Roll Reprobate /
Lou Brutus.
Description: Los Angeles: Rare Bird Books, 2020.
Identifiers: LCCN 2019051732 | ISBN 9781644280768 (hardback)
Subjects: LCSH: Brutus, Lou, 1962– | Disc jockeys—United
States—Biography. | Radio personalities—United States—Biography. |
Rock musicians—Anecdotes. | LCGFT: Autobiographies.
Classification: LCC ML429.B88 A3 2020 |
DDC 782.42166092 [B]—dc23

LC record available at https://lccn.loc.gov/2019051732

*For Mom and Dad because they let me go to
all the shows that I wanted to.*

*For Pearl, Licedog, Bud, and Finster because they never
said "NO" to seeing bands.*

*For Bert Berendt because I'll always be sad that
he never got to a concert.*

*For Dan Ingram because he was
the best DJ who ever lived.*

*For the tour managers because they
never get enough thanks.*

*For Geri, Jilly, and Darla the Pup because
I'd always rather be home.*

"All the world's a stage they say
And I've seen many things
Standing with my little ukulele in the wings"

—Neil Innes, "My Little Ukulele"

FOREWORD

BY COREY TAYLOR

IF YOU EVER WANT to become the world's most envious person, play this simple game with Lou Brutus: "Hey, Did You Ever See (Insert Your Favorite Band) Live?" Not only will it turn out that he has indeed seen your favorite band live, he's either A) Seen them open up for Led Zeppelin/ Aerosmith/Kiss/Cheap Trick, or B) Seen them play in the coolest, smallest, most intimate setting imaginable...TWICE. It's enough to make you want to leave the conversation entirely, if you weren't already completely rapt in excitement and fascination.

The first time I met my friend Lou, I was under doctor's orders to engage in vocal rest because of damage I'd done to my chords during a Slipknot rehearsal. It turned out that THAT would stand me in good stead since Lou wasn't going to let me get a word in edgewise anyway, whether I was cleared for speech or not. He is, and has always been, one of the most interesting people to talk to on any subject. Need an awesome book to read? He's got a recommendation. Looking for the latest in cool music? He's got the band for you. Want a new venue to visit while in a host of major cities? He's got it dialed, along with the radio station promoting the event and the DJ making the on-stage announcement—that is, if it doesn't turn out to be Lou himself.

Lou Brutus is not only an amazing glimpse into what rock radio was, he's also the marker for what it's become, and what it still may be. And this is because of his greatest strength: his total and unapologetic love for rock/metal/punk/you name it. It's clear from his descriptions of songs to his details on where he was when he heard them performed for the first time. It's a gift. Lou's stories—and there are SO MANY—aren't just a man reporting from the front. With Brutus, you're in the moment WITH him. It's conspiratorial. He's trusting that you're as dedicated to "The Club"—meaning all the music and the people who play it—as he is. This isn't robotic recall; this is robust recollection. He's a touchstone for the days when rock concerts, big and small, were still the Wild West. They were Barnum & Bailey, the times of Grant and McGhee. His insight makes it all so special, however. The fan inside you is given a voice reflected in the fan inside him. He makes you a part of the audience, and you relish the way he sets the tone.

He's made friends with some of his favorite artists over the years, and it shows when he's simultaneously regaling you with a good story AND complimenting a good buddy. That's what music means to Lou: it isn't a commodity, it's a connection. I've enjoyed his stories for twenty years, and now I hope you enjoy them too. So dig in, Fair Reader. Go forth and wreak havoc.

Oh, and Lou—TELL THEM NOT TO FORGET THE FUCKING GOLF SHOES!!

PREFACE

SOME OF MY EARLIEST *memories revolve around music. When I was very young—six or seven—I became enamored of The Beatles. As they were famously first introduced to the United States on* The Ed Sullivan Show, *I would dutifully sit on the parquet floor of our living room in front of the television with my family each Sunday night hoping for them to appear. Sullivan's show was the top-rated "variety" program in the country, presenting a wide mix of entertainers including actors, comedians, musicians, jugglers, and animal acts. You never knew what you'd see. I would then spend the week mimicking whatever I'd viewed, telling my folks I'd be on the show some day. It was during one viewing of the program that my dad spoke to me from his reserved spot on the sofa.*

"Son, be the pointer."

"What do you mean, Dad?"

"Every week on the show there are all sorts of entertainers. They come and go. It's not steady work. However, Ed Sullivan is there every week, and all he does is point at the acts as they come out. He doesn't need any talent, and he gets a steady

paycheck just for pointing. So if you're thinking about show business...be the pointer."

So essentially, that's what I do for a living. I'm a pointer. I point out good music. I point out good movies. I point to the band coming onstage.

My old man was pretty smart.

OVERTURE: WHO DOES WHAT?

A PRIMER ON THE JOBS OF THE MUSIC BUSINESS

LIKE ANY OTHER BUSINESS, rock and roll has a division of labor. There are a host of jobs, and each one entails something unique. The difference here is that rock and roll has more people getting blowjobs in the bathroom during business hours while simultaneously doing lines of coke off the ass of whoever is doing the blowing than most other branches of industry. Well, except maybe Wall Street.

Here is a list of the more common music industry positions dealt with in this book.

LEAD SINGER: The person out in front of the band. Not always the smartest human in the group, except when it comes to getting laid. The large percentage of them fill up any room they enter with happy excitement. They are charismatic beyond normal human expectation. However, a small number of lead singers are black holes that suck the souls of those around them in their never-ending bid to be the center of the universe. There aren't a lot of those types, but there are some.

LEAD GUITARIST: This is someone who locked themselves in their bedroom at a very young age to learn how to play along with all of their favorite songs. Many of them suffer a paleness of skin due to this from which they'll never recover. (Jack White, I'm looking at you.) The weaker members of this position just continue to ape the guitarist who influenced them the most while growing up. The better ones build upon what they've learned in order to forge their own unique style. The best of them make you go, "How the fuck do they play like that?" The lead guitarist is often locked in a battle for control of the band with the lead singer. Pride would never allow the lead guitarist to admit this. The lead singer usually doesn't say anything about these disagreements, as he or she is too busy charming the fuck out of the world.

RHYTHM GUITARIST: A real mixed bag. Some are just glad to be here. Others are the heart and soul of their group. In a few cases, it's actually the rhythm player calling all the shots. The best representation of all this was Malcolm Young of AC/DC. Make no mistake, it was always Malcolm's band. He was the brains behind AC/DC. Besides, no rhythm guitarist should be taken lightly, because anyone who can successfully navigate between the lead singer and the lead guitarist is a force to be reckoned with.

BASS PLAYER: It would be very easy to shrug off bass players. However, Gene Simmons of KISS and Paul McCartney of The Beatles are bass players, so that right there tells you not to underestimate these four-string mother-pluckers. In some cases, the bass player is an incredible talent, like John Entwistle of The Who or Tony Levin of King Crimson/Peter Gabriel. In others, they're the least talented but most driven, with the strongest desire to be in a band. It's my belief that in their formative years, those particular players struck rock-star poses with their guitar in the mirror far more often than lead guitarists did, which led to them falling behind in actual playing ability. No, I'm serious. Please note, I *tried* to be a bass player when I was around thirteen years old but sucked worse than anyone in history.

KEYBOARDISTS: There aren't many of them compared to the other members and those that are in the business are usually too busy with their pain-in-the-ass gear to be seen very often.

DRUMMER: Usually, the true life of the party is the drummer. The physical nature of their job leads them to need to let off the most steam after a gig, which causes all sorts of fun stupidity. At the top of the list is one person I never saw whom I wish I had: Keith Moon, the drummer for The Who. He was an amazing showman and legendary partier. Too bad it killed him. One thing to watch closely about drummers is how their style of play affects their health later in life. For example, Max Weinberg of the E Street Band plays heavily with his hands and his wrists, which has led to medical problems and hand horrors. Morgan Rose of Sevendust puts his back into his playing and, sure enough, it's led to back problems for him. I hope to one day open a medical facility for drummers only, though I doubt the nurses would be safe.

TOUR MANAGER: The music industry equivalent of a Den Mother in the Cub Scouts. It's the tour manager (or TM) who actually has to keep the rock and roll circus moving. The TM is the responsible adult. The one who has to do all the work and keep everyone focused. If something fucks up, it's the TM's fault. If everything goes smoothly, it's the band that gets all the credit. Especially the lead singer. If you need something done on a concert tour or at a festival show, go right to the tour manager. Just remember to do whatever they say because if you fuck up with the TM, you will not be invited back. The TM is also in charge of the passes. Tread lightly with them.

TOURING ROADIES: These are the professional roadies who travel with the group. Some are specialized in areas like sound or lighting while others "tech" for a guitarist or drummer. Many work full time for one band, one musician, or a particular management company that handles numerous groups. Martin Connors, who has guitar teched for Jim Root of Slipknot, and others, is an amazing professional and one of my fave people to see on the road. The touring roadies are usually the backbone of any concert trek and generally the most fun of anybody on it. Touring roadies are the best people to ask for guitar picks, drumsticks, set lists, etc. They have a girl in every town. And she has friends. All of the touring roadie's clothing is black. All of it.

LOCAL CREW: This is the toughest gig in rock and roll. These are local men and women who are hired for larger concert tours that come into town. They are there to move road cases. That's about it. The pay ain't great, but they do get to see the show for free—though they're usually too tired to watch so just don't give a fuck. Best perk of the job is customized tour T-shirts that only go to local crew. These shirts are often exchanged at the concert for cocaine and/or blowjobs. (Seriously, much of the economy of a concert tour is based upon a currency of oral sex and runny noses. Well, at least in the old days.) The very best artists tip the local crew well. There are not enough "very best" artists. It is the local crew members who are the most likely to have STDs.

DRIVER: Newer, or "baby" bands, tour in vans and drive themselves. That sucks. There's no place to sleep, and the van smells like feet. More on **that** later in this tome. The biggest touring bands go by plane, but most go by bus. Each bus has a driver. Most of these drivers are from the South and are batshit crazy. They also treat the bus like it's a human extension of themselves, so don't fuck anything up in their bus. The driver isn't often around as there are strict laws about the amount of sleep they must get, so while the band may go days or weeks without a room, the driver is usually snoozing away in a nearby hotel.

GROUPIES: First, I must state that every industry has its groupies. The music industry just happens to have some of the most depraved. It is my sincere belief that everyone you meet should be treated with respect—unless they prove themselves unworthy of it, however, and that includes groupies. There are all kinds of groupies. Some are nice, clean, local girls (and sometimes guys) who just wanna hang out with a slight element of rock 'n' roll danger. Other groupies have their sights set on getting with a band member, sometimes dreaming of a long-term relationship. Then, of course, you have some who just wanna be as fucking nasty as they can. These maniacal manipulators of musical meat —immortalized in the song "Crew Slut" by the late Frank Zappa—will generally do anything with anybody wearing a backstage pass. There actually aren't nearly as many of these as you think. I always found it very easy to deal with groupies once I learned early on that under no circumstances would any of them ever be interested in a radio DJ (see below). After I figured that out, I realized that groupies were often the best-informed people on a tour and therefore could often be useful founts of knowledge. Many of them have serious jobs and careers. Rock 'n' roll just happens to be where they get their freak on and let out stress. Ain't nothing wrong with that.

MANAGEMENT: These are the folks who make a piece, usually between fifteen and twenty percent, of everything that a band grosses. Many of them manage lots of bands, guiding every facet of their entire career. And they don't have to smell feet all night. Take one guess who the smartest people in the music biz are.

RECORD COMPANY PEOPLE: The men and women who work for record companies. There used to be a lot of them, but now there are very few. It's their job to contact radio stations to convince them that the music their company releases should be played on the air. When a band signed to the record company comes to town, the record company people are there to facilitate the group's interaction with radio and fans. There used to be a representative for every recording company in every large market. That was before the record companies fucked up the whole download thing, forcing fans to create their own—albeit illegal—system, and the bottom dropped out of the industry. These days one person may cover huge portions of the country. The good fallout from that is that most of the weasel types have been pushed out, leaving a higher percentage of quality people in these gigs. Another part of their job is to buy drinks for everybody. All night, every night. They *used* to send radio people like me tons of free albums, now they just send download links. Fuckers.

PROGRAM DIRECTORS: The person in charge of the content on the radio station, all the way from the DJs who are hired to what music gets played. The program director, or PD, will often stand through an entire concert as their ass is chafed from the constant kissing it receives because they can help make or break a record or band. They also decide on carrying shows like mine, AND THAT MAKES THEM THE MOST AWESOME MEN AND WOMEN IN THE HISTORY OF WESTERN CIVILIZATION!!!

RADIO DJs: The guy from the local radio station who sometimes gets to go onstage at a concert in between bands and shout into a microphone for up to thirty seconds. There is no sex, very few drugs, but plenty of rock 'n' roll for these people. You will learn more about the shame and degradation involved in this position throughout this book.

THE TIME I ATTENDED MY FIRST CONCERT & THREW UP ON CARLOS SANCHEZ

IT WAS AT MY first ever concert—Black Sabbath and Ted Nugent at Madison Square Garden on December 6, 1976— that I threw up on Carlos Sanchez.

Carlos was dating my older sister, Patti, and I had convinced them to let me tag along to the concert in New York City. We lived in Manalapan Township, just outside of Englishtown, New Jersey, so it was a one-hour jaunt on the bus.

I woke that Monday feeling woozy with flu-like symptoms, but I knew I was a dead man with no parental permission to attend the show that night if I stayed home from class. I was in my freshman year at Manalapan High School at the time. I suppose it was a fairly typical school, with fairly typical students who thought fairly typically about wanting to be anywhere other than there as they dry humped one another against the lockers in the hallways between classes. Basically, everyone looked like cast members from *That '70s Show*, except with more pimples.

23

We boarded the bus to New York from a commuter stop along Highway 9 late that afternoon. Yes, the very same Highway 9 immortalized by Bruce Springsteen in "Born to Run." Oddly enough, as he grew up just a few miles away from me in Freehold, New Jersey, he's the one rock star I haven't met. He certainly wasn't on the bus that day as we rumbled north, onto the New Jersey Turnpike, through the Lincoln Tunnel, and into Port Authority, where it disgorged us into Manhattan. This foreshadowed my own disgorging later in the night.

I would make that same bus run hundreds of times in my life for both concerts and work in later years. I always thought of the bus fare as if it were the admission price to an evil amusement park. It would have been cool to turn the Lincoln and Holland Tunnel entrances from Jersey to New York into spooky gates like for a haunted ride. Maybe it could've said "Welcome to Satan World" over the top and been adorned with devilish hookers, pimps, and drug dealers.

In those days the walk down Eighth Avenue from the bus depot at Port Authority to Madison Square Garden took you past blocks filled with sleazy porn palaces that sold the nastiest skin mags on the planet, as well as various sexual devices like vibrators the size of missile launchers that looked like they could be used to shake the jets then flying for the Soviet Union right out of the sky. They also featured little booths where you could flagellate yourself into a frothing, heterosexual frenzy, while peering through a peephole at a naked lady. The Tubes would use this slippery, protein-enriched scenario just a few years later as the basis for a hit song entitled "She's a Beauty."

My sister simply said, "Don't touch anything or speak to anyone," as we walked in a tight group, and I mopped the sweat from my fevered brow. She needn't have told me, as I was already trying not to come in contact with anything for fear of picking up and dying from a horrible venereal disease before I actually managed to get myself laid for the first time.

This was the backdrop as we made our way to "The Garden," as it was lovingly known to generations of New Yorkers who lined up there by the millions through the years to see the Rangers, Knicks, and boxing matches, as well as countless other entertainment events. As we walked closer to the arena, the businesses slowly morphed from sex boutiques to bars, pubs, and fast food restaurants that even the cities sneering, oversized rats would have thought twice about dining in. The streets began to clog with longhaired, red-eyed, marijuana-smellin' Black Sabbath fans.

There were also lots and lots of guys hawking black concert T-shirts.

Purchasing one's first ever black concert T-shirt was an important rite of passage for all music fans. The black concert T-shirt was your not-so-subtle message to the world around you regarding your discerning taste in music. Most importantly, it allowed you bragging rights in school the next day, as if saying, "While you were watching *Happy Days* with your mommy and daddy, I was listening to Ozzy Osbourne bring down hellfire upon my immortal soul, you pussy."

I bought a bootlegged Black Sabbath shirt with a red dragon on it. For two bucks. It was all my budget would allow as the "official" concert T's were out of my beggar man price range at an astronomical six dollars. It turned out to be one of the greatest bargains of my young life, as that cheap-o shirt would end up lasting me through many years and hundreds of washings.

Speaking of prices, let's talk about our tickets for that night. We were to sit directly across the length of the arena from the stage about mid-way up, the green section of the color-coded Garden seating in those days. The price? Six dollars and fifty cents. I'll repeat that. Six dollars and fifty fuckin' cents. For a live concert. Yeah, I know. The "convenience charge" those fucking fucks at the ticket services rob you of nowadays is five times that alone. And we weren't even in the cheapest seats as the nosebleed blue section up top was only five dollars and fifty cents. One can only imagine the Darwinian bouillabaisse of humanity in the accursed upper deck during a Black Sabbath concert in 1976. Unzipping one's fly before taking a piss was probably optional for some of these degenerate yahoos, given their chemically altered states. Of course, we weren't down on the floor or in the red or yellow sections for, as my sister's boyfriend said, "I'll be damned if I'm ever going to pay seven fifty for a concert ticket!"

Anyway, we stepped up to the hallowed entryway of Madison Square Garden, which incidentally is actually round, and handed our tickets to the uniformed usher at the turnstile. He didn't say anything as he ripped our tickets and handed us our stubs. He didn't have to. He gave us the same look he was giving everyone that night. A look that seemed to say, "If every one of you dirty, heathen, godless, devil-worshipping, drug-gobbling little bastards chokes on your own vomit before the end of the night and is sent directly to Hades to be forcibly sodomized by Satan himself for all of eternity, it will be too good for you." So much for him being thankful to us for helping provide him with a livelihood. He certainly didn't know how close his wish was to coming true for yours truly.

A quick note here about the ticket stub itself. It was a typical red, white, and blue Ticketmaster stub from the time. It's certainly nothing special to look at. Actually, it's rather disappointing as at that point in time the ushers gave you the short end of the stub, only about a quarter of the original ticket. All of the info at the center of the ducat, including the artist name and venue, was taken away from you. That's made ID'ing stubs from this time a bit harder for me, but in the case of this ticket, I'd know it anywhere. It's my first. You never forget your first ticket stub. I still like to take it out of storage now and then to play it some Black Sabbath music for old time's sake. No, really. By the way, have I mentioned yet how crushingly dull my personal life is?

Now, I want you to remember that during the bus travel, foot slog on the streets of New York and entryway into the show, I was as sick as the proverbial dog, pale as a ghost, and sweating like Meatloaf staring down a platter of deep-fried Ho-Hos. Luckily, the excitement of the day was pumping enough extra adrenaline into me to keep the forward momentum going in my Chuck Taylors.

We then made our way up the seemingly endless line of escalators that carried us to our perch in the hall, where the floor was already littered with discarded cans of beer, stubbed out Marlboro cigarette butts, and hot dog wrappers, as well as a few already overly medicated fans who'd passed out on the chilly cement, dreaming sweet dreams of leather-clad groupies and stomach pumps.

While I was bewildered by the assault of sights, sounds, and smells in the concrete hallways, Carlos and my sister coolly navigated me through it all and we finally walked through the gateway and into the main hall of Madison Square Garden.

The current Madison Square Garden is the fourth building in New York City to have that name, the first rose up in 1879, while the current one was built in 1968 with a major renovation in 1991. It seats approximately 20,000 people for a concert. I honestly believe it to be the most famous and awesome hall on the planet. Everyone needs to have a thrilling experience inside of it at least once in his or her lifetime.

I finally took my first steps into the main hall of this massive, modern marvel of twentieth-century architecture, this tribute to man's enduring desire to gather in large numbers to witness both sport and art at its finest, this stone and steel embodiment of humanity's quest for excellence, and my first thought was, "Holy fuck. It's a giant cloud of pot smoke."

I shit you not. I could not see to the other side of the arena for the thick haze of marijuana that had been slowly wheezed from the lungs of the glassy-eyed concertgoers as they awaited the band.

Back in the day, the ushers couldn't be bothered with stopping people from smoking weed. Smoking cigarettes in most places indoors was still fine and dandy. While smoking dope was illegal, some poor schmuck in a Madison Square Garden blazer, armed with nothing more than a flashlight, wasn't about to risk life and limb charging into an arena full of drug-crazed miscreants who were there to hear tender songs of love like "Sabbath Bloody Sabbath" for the then current minimum wage of $2.30. Nowadays, of course, if you fire up a ciggy at a show they'll beat the living fuck out of you and prosecute you as if you were the second coming of Charles Manson. Yes, it's made things healthier, but it's certainly taken away a little bit of the danger, and with it the fun, of attending concerts. However, less cancer is always a plus!

After the initial shock of seeing the entire 1976 crop of Columbian dirt weed exhaled into one place wore off, I was able to get my bearings and find my way to my very own molded green plastic fold-down chair next to Patti and her boyfriend.

Section 342. Row G. Seat 11.

Soon after, the house lights went down, the crowd roared, and Ted Nugent hit the stage. At that time, Ted wasn't all that well-known on the East Coast. We knew he was some crazy-assed, wild man from Detroit, which was about the extent of our knowledge. I knew nothing of his earlier career in the Amboy Dukes, and his second solo record, *Free-For-All*, had just been issued the month before. As best as I can remember, he began his set by leaping out over the top of his drummer and landing in a split at the center of the stage, all while coaxing shrieking notes out of his Gibson hollow-bodied guitar. He looked like a cave man that had stepped out of a time machine fresh off of banging Betty Rubble. Doggy-style. While Barney watched.

My initial reaction was something akin to, "YEEEE-AAAAHHHHHHHMOTHERFUCKERRRRRRRRYEEEEEEE-AHHHHHHHHHHOOOOOWWWWWWWOOOOOHH-HHHHHHHHHHFUCKYEAHWOOOOOOOFUCKING-HOOOOWHOOOOOOOOOARRRRRRRGGGGGGGGHH-HHHHHH!!!!!"

No matter what else happened the rest of the night, I was hooked. I was going to be a lifer. I was going to see every concert I could. It was like being struck by lightning. It was instantaneous. Everything else in life up till then seemed bland and gray in comparison. I knew where I belonged. Here. In the crowd. At a rock show.

To this day, even after thousands of shows, I still get that butterfly feeling in my stomach when the lights go down and a band hits the stage. It's more alluring than any drug. Plus, it doesn't give you a nosebleed like cocaine does, unless the guy next to you throws his fist in the air when he hears his favorite song and accidentally socks you in the schnoz.

This was years before Ted Nugent went batshit crazy with politics. On this night in December 1976 there was no talk of current events, he simply called down the power of whatever rock gods there are who smile favorably upon those artists who wear a raccoon tail, swing across stage on a vine, and shoot flaming arrows past their bassist. Nuanced? No. Entertaining? Yes. Oh, yes.

Ted's set was short but intense with my personal favorite of his numbers being "Dog, Dog, Doggy Dog," which I didn't discover for another week or two was actually entitled with the far more sinister moniker of "Dog Eat Dog."

Sadly, my night had now reached its apex and would soon degenerate into a nauseating pit of unpleasantness. After Ted's set there was a loooong intermission. Why so long? I never found out. Rumor had it that Black Sabbath was afraid to follow Nugent after his ass-kicking set. At least this is what Ted later claimed when I first interviewed him years later. Legend has it that Ozzy and Sabbath guitarist Tony Iommi were brawling backstage. Frank Zappa, whom I would later get to know and who intro'd the band that night, put it down to technical difficulties when he brought them onstage. Whatever the reason, the long intermission coupled with a Ted Nugent fueled rush of adrenaline that momentarily banished my flu-ish feelings had convinced me that it was a good idea to start guzzling from a bottle of Boone's Farm Strawberry Wine.

Ahhh, Boone's Farm. The preferred wine of mid-seventies rock fans on a budget. So overly sweetened that one could fall into a diabetic coma after just a few sips. Often in those days, though not in this case, served out of a leather wine sack that gave it the savory sapidity of unwashed goat ass. So lowly in the world of the cheap buzz that even the mid-Manhattan vagabonds would turn their noses up if given a choice between it and something more highbrow like Mad Dog 20/20 or Night Train. The champagne of twist-cap wines? I think not.

However, it was this bottle of pigwash, smuggled into the venue in the sleeve of Carlos's brown Marlboro Man jacket, that taught me my first important lesson in concert attendance, a deterrent example that I would carry with me for the rest of my life. Hard-learned knowledge that I will now share with you in the hope that it will carry you safely through your own years of festival attendance: If you have the flu, guzzling down an entire bottle of shitty wine in one throw is a really, *really* bad idea.

Yup, sickness and all, I tilted back my head and slammed down the entire bottle. I drank like a real man. Like a grizzled concert veteran. Like a rock soldier. In other words, like a fucking idiot.

It was as if I was Indiana Jones replacing the golden idol with the bag of sand. Initially, I smugly thought I had made a wise decision, only to feel an ungodly rumbling a few moments later that told me otherwise.

Carlos and my sister chuckled as my head drooped forward and my chin said a drunken "how do ya do" to my chest.

All of Madison Square Garden began to slowly spin around me. I closed my eyes, but that only made it worse. I finally settled on leaving them open just a slit to get some sense of the horizon. Sweat poured from my brow. My limbs quivered. The liquefied fruit of Boone's Farm called out for release like demonic grapes of wrath trapped in the fiery hell of my belly. Then, everything went black. I thought I had gone blind and let out a self-pitying moan that seemed to rise to a cacophony in my ears. Turns out it was the lights going down, the crowed going nuts, and Black Sabbath taking the stage.

What were they like? How was the show? You are asking the wrong dumbass. I was gripping the armrests of my chair and holding on for dear life, so the performance was the least of my concerns. The only thing that I seem to remember of their set was Ozzy Osbourne leaping around the stage like a white satin-clad Spider-Man, his prowess aided by the spiderlike fact that he had four legs and four arms. "No, that can't be right," I slurred to myself. Wait. Seeing double. Focus. Focus. Only two legs. Cool. Two legs good, four legs bad.

And with that, I passed out.

Believe you me when I tell you that dark are the dreams of a fourteen-year-old wino's slumber when accompanied by lyrics like "evil souls fall to hell, ever trapped in burning cells" as visions of blue-seated, unwashed dopers urinating in their own tighty-whities dance through their head.

Finally, after what seemed like an ungodly eternity sung about in one of their tunes, Sabbath's twelve-song set was over. The lights came up. My sister and Carlos shook me out of my stupor, helped me to my feet, and we made our way toward the exit, which would take us back down the escalators and into the chilly December air.

However, fate and the E. & J. Gallo Winery, the manufacturer of Boone's Farm Strawberry Wine, had conspired together to make our escape more eventful than anyone had hoped for. The flu-wracked contents of my innards had awoken with me and they too wished for release. Quickly. I felt the burst of activity as they bade a fond farewell to the lining of my stomach wall and began their rise to freedom like Steve McQueen on a motorcycle speeding over a mass of barbed wire away from a German POW camp.

The dark realization came to me that I had but seconds before the wine burst forth from me like a vociferously volcanic Vesuvius of vomit. A realization made even more unpleasant by the fact we were jammed in like sardines among the other concert refugees and that Carlos baby-stepped less than a foot in front of me, so I had no room to wretch.

I couldn't speak to warn Carlos as I had clenched my throat muscles to try to slow the great escape from my esophagus. However, I had to do something to warn him, so I did the only thing my alcohol-addled brain could think of in that flash. I tugged on the sleeve of his brown jacket. This, I instinctively knew, would cause him to immediately leap out of the way and allow me a clear lane to empty the ill-fated contents of stomach.

Well, it didn't work out that way. You see, when you tug on someone's jacket, they stop dead in their tracks to look behind them to ask you what the hell you want. And that's just what he did.

"What the hell do you want?" asked Carlos.

"BROOOOOOOOOOOWERRRRRRROUF," I replied.

A torrent of spew shot forth from my pie hole. A veritable geyser of cheap wine so powerful I could have taken on Old

Faithful that night and been victorious four falls out of five. If I had pointed my mouth up to the sky there's a fair chance my upchuck would have knocked out the recently launched Marisat F3 satellite from its geosynchronous orbit around the Earth. Certainly the US Navy, who had sent it into space, would think they had just entered a new and dangerously disgusting arms race with the Russians.

In only a second, I had managed to soak Carlos's entire arm in thick goo that smelled like rancid strawberries.

"You idiot," he said.

I leaned forward to wretch some more. The weight of my head, thrust so far forward, would normally have caused me to careen forward and onto my face but the force of the next liquid projectile actually acted as the third leg of a human tripod that kept me up as I staggered forward to balance myself against a payphone on the wall.

Carlos asked, "Who the hell are you calling?"

"GRRRRREEEERRRROOOOOWWWWWERRR," I barked as I gave the phone a shower so thick that the receiver probably stank of my insides for the rest of the basketball and hockey seasons at the Garden that winter. The change slot of the unfortunate phone would to this day have a residual pool of my gastrointestinal juices if it still hangs.

Carlos now gripped the scruff of my neck and led me toward the men's room, holding me at arm's length like a heaving marionette. He may or may not have used my skull to open the door headfirst; one could hardly have blamed him if he did. As I staggered in and tried to steady myself, I took a glance around the white porcelain room. I realized that I was surrounded by dozens of other young men from the Greater

34

New York Metropolitan area and that each and every one of them was puking his fucking brains out.

There were guys puking in the toilets. Some were puking in 'em two at a time. There were others on their knees, puking into the urinals, their faces slapped back by the triple bonus stench of vomit, piss, and urinal cake. Still more puked right into the sinks. Even the guys who didn't walk in to puke started to puke, overcome as they were by the pathetic peristaltic pyrotechnics. The grim emesistic statistics rose by the second.

The bleached walls spun around me as droplets of booze and chunks of chewed hot dog pieces flew by. I dodged it all as best I could, cleaned myself up quickly, and then stumbled back out into the relative sanity of the hallway.

How I made it home that night, I have no memory. I can only guess my sister guided me like Lucy led Linus out of the predawn pumpkin patch to finally collapse fully clothed, facedown in bed.

The next day, I walked somewhat unsteadily into school wearing my two-dollar Black Sabbath T-shirt with the red dragon on it.

A friend ran up and asked, "How was it?"

I told him the God's honest truth about the entire night. "It was fucking awesome."

THE TIME I WENT TO THE ARCTIC AND GOT IN A MOSH PIT WITH A BUNCH OF KIDS IN POLAR BEAR FUR WHILE METALLICA SANG ABOUT SODOMIZING A GOAT

IN THE SUMMER OF 1995, I was hosting the afternoon drive shift at WRCX-FM in Chicago when I was called into Program Director Dave Richard's office to answer a question.

"How would you like to fly to the shores of the Arctic Ocean to see Metallica do a private show in an Eskimo village?

I told him, "Ya gotta get off the drugs, son. Ya gotta get off the drugs."

However, he was sober and sincere.

The show, perhaps the most over-the-top publicity stunt for a beer brand in the history of mankind's long, slobbering love affair with alcohol, was to be called "The Molson Ice Polar Beach Party." The plan was to pick five hundred contest winners from across the United States and Canada, then fly them to the very edge of civilization for an invitation-only concert by Metallica, Hole, Veruca Salt, and Moist.

Gee, a thousand miles from anywhere, triangulated between the fiercest metal band on the planet, Courtney

Love, and man-eating polar bears? What could possibly go wrong? I immediately said, "Fuck, yeah."

Actually, I didn't know if there would really be polar bears there. Up to that point, my only knowledge of Arctic flora and fauna came from my seasonal viewings of the old Rankin/Bass holiday special *Rudolph the Red-Nosed Reindeer*. After considering it for a moment, I doubted Metallica would be rocking covers of "Jingle, Jingle, Jingle" or "We Are Santa's Elves," although I believe to this day they could have pulled off a credible version of "We're a Couple of Misfits." Think of their version as a brooding lament in the style of their hit "Nothing Else Matters." On second thought, don't.

I was chosen as the lone media representative from the US to attend the gig. I'm not sure whether it was because I had a long history of covering historic Metallica concerts or because I'd be missed the least in case someone needed to be sacrificed to some fierce Arctic beast akin to a wampa from the ice planet Hoth in *Star Wars*.

This show would lead to one of the finest concert moments I ever experienced as well as begin my relationship with one of the grossest rock songs ever written.

The concert was going to be held in a place named Tuktoyaktuk, so the first order of business for me was to learn just how the fuck to correctly pronounce the name "Tuktoyaktuk" on the air. The village, thankfully called "Tuk" for short, can be found on the north coast of mainland Canada in the Northwest Territories on the shores of the Beaufort Sea, which leads out to the greater Arctic Ocean. It gets its name from local legend wherein it is written, on whatever it is that they write it on up there, a native woman saw several caribou wade into the water and become petrified. My guess is that they froze their furry balls off, as the average temperature there is just a bit higher than the brainwave activity levels of the typical *Keeping Up with the Kardashians* viewer. For our Labor Day weekend excursion, we could expect temps around freezing. Yippee.

How do you get to Tuktoyaktuk? Well, to drive there, just take Canada's Dempster Highway to its end at Inuvik. Then wait for winter to arrive and the MacKenzie River to freeze. When it does, drive north on the river through untold miles of death-filled Arctic tundra known as the Tuktoyaktuk Winter Road (later made famous on the television program *Ice Road Truckers*), and fight off any marauding bands of Arctic wolves with a taste for human flesh. Try not to get lost, which could lead to you dying alone in the barren wilderness crying out for God's mercy on your pathetic soul. Then bang a right when you get to the Beaufort Sea, and pull into Tuk.

In other words, it's better to have a plane and a more acute sense of direction than Amelia Earhart.

We would be flown from the States up to Inuvik, which was the only town in that part of the hemisphere that had the facilities to handle visits from so many people at one time. We'd spend a couple of days there to sightsee, attend some Molson-sponsored parties, drink several gullets full of free beer, then fly up to Tuk and back the day of the concert. After which we would turn tail and head south before the whole joint started looking like the Ice Queen's palace in Narnia.

In the months preceding the concert, I was registering listeners to join me on my trek. One person would be chosen who could bring a guest. The reaction to the contesting was insane as Metallica at this time, after establishing themselves as the top group in the metal genre, were exploding in the mainstream to become the biggest band on the planet. Add to that that it was an invite-only performance in the most exotic location in North America that still had electricity to run guitar amps, and you had a recipe for heavy metal, ape-shit behavior. Their biggest hit to date had been "Enter Sandman," and I was going off to a frozen Never-Never Land with them.

The inclusion of Courtney Love's band Hole added to the feeling of madness. The group's reputation was that of a walking, talking, dope-shooting car wreck. Tales of their drug use—whether true or not—had already become legend. Visions of a drug-addled Courtney with a bone knife clenched in between blood-drenched teeth as she stalked musk ox in the frozen latitudes, clad only in virgin walrus fur, danced in my head.

I knew Veruca Salt quite well, as they were a local Chicago band. They were also my first on-air celebrity crush. I often wrote lovelorn poetry for the group's two singer/guitarists Nina Gordon and Louise Post, which I would read on-air. This schtick would be the forerunner to my over-the-airwaves, mostly imaginary—okay, totally imaginary—love affair with Lzzy Hale of Halestorm years later.

Not surprisingly, this did not go over really big with my wife, who sneeringly referred to them as "Veruca Sluts." That I would be traipsing off to parts unknown with them went over about as well as an egg fart in a crowded igloo. It led to some awkward conversations at home...

What's for dinner, honey? *I don't know. Why not ask your Arctic hump buddies to defrost some frozen whore food for you?*

Feeling frisky? *Not really. You should just try humping your northern snow trollops.*

Who did John F. Kennedy defeat in the 1960 presidential election? *I'm not sure, dear. Perhaps it was one of those guitar-playing harlots you plan on finger-banging when you get to Fukaslutfuk.*

Ahhh, domestic bliss.

(EDITOR'S NOTE: Lou's wife disavows each of the preceding quotes. He sticks by them, saying, "Well, that's how I remember it.")

The last group for the show was Moist, a band from Vancouver, BC, with a strong singer named David Usher and which gave the bill a bit of a Canadian flavor. The day would rock for damn sure. How could it not? Besides, getting away from home at this point seemed like a good idea as my wife was giving me a shoulder colder than Ernest Borgnine's ass in *Ice Station Zebra*.

At Dave Richard's suggestion, I had begun to look for someone who lived up in Tuktoyaktuk who could provide some on-air background to the upcoming trip. With no other ideas, I finally contacted the Royal Canadian Mounted Police and asked if they had an officer up there. They put me through to Constable Dave Dirksen. His thick Canadian accent and matter-of-fact take on this massive show coming to his tiny enclave was a hit with the listeners in Chicago. His reports basically just described the everyday life of any small town—his just happened to have Metallica coming to it. We'd send him tapes of his daily updates and he'd play them over the police radio for the other constables spread out over the far north, many of whom would provide security at the concert. Besides being entertaining radio, I figured this was also prudent travel behavior as it's always good to align yourself with armed individuals when traveling to places where humans aren't quite at the top of the food chain.

At the airport prior to the departure of our charter to Inuvik, the contest winners from around North America began to gather. It was quite an interesting cross section of people. Some were über-scary metal fans, but most just looked like regular rockers with the wide, telltale grins of people who were getting a once in a lifetime trip on somebody else's dime. Others sported the egg-sized pupils of those who had planned on smuggling drugs over an international border, chickened out, and ate their entire stash in an airport restroom. I suppose a few of them brought something illicit, but I didn't. Call me old-fashioned, but I was brought up to believe that a man's rectum is no place for a baggie full of dope.

As I recall, there were two separate planes. Ours went straight to Inuvik, while the other had a refueling stop in Yellow Knife. I was kinda jealous our flight didn't stop there, as Yellow Knife sounded like a place name from the early, white box *Dungeons & Dragons* rules. The trip up was fun. Plenty of free beer, a bit of crowd-surfing over the seats, and a few couples who joined the Mile-High Club as the rest of us pounded on the restroom door outside while they pounded on the inside.

My joking request to enter the cockpit, take the plane over the North Pole, and "bomb those commie fucks in Russia back to the Stone Age" was grimly denied by the pilots. The stewardess stopped filling my drink orders after that.

No band members were on either of these flights. They had gone ahead separately. Chances were we would not see them until show day in Tuk.

That night we landed in Inuvik and immediately watched our fingers and toes turn blue from the cold. The blue actually matched the color of the Molson labels. Wow. Their marketing guys really had thought of everything.

The ironic part about this whole fucking blowout was that it was going to be held in a town where the selling of alcohol is illegal. Even in Inuvik, where Molson sponsored outdoor beer blasts for us, booze is strictly regulated, the reason being that alcohol does not mix well with the natives of the area.

The aboriginal people of Inuvik and Tuktoyaktuk are Inuit (aka Inuvialuit). To be honest, I don't think any of them are crazy about being referred to as an "Eskimo." They're part of the related folk who populate the top of the planet, strung out along Greenland, Canada, Russia, and other places where the branches only grow on one side of the trees 'cause the wind is constantly blowing from the other. Shit, Tuk doesn't even *have* any trees. It's not only above the Arctic Circle, it's above the tree line and nothing grows higher than your shin. Dope harvesting, popular in Vancouver, is obviously not going to become a growth industry in this section of Canada until global warming kicks into high gear.

We did see some scattered drunkenness among the native people in Inuvik. Some of the men were so stewed that they were stumbling around incoherent in the middle of the day. I mean raving and drooling kinda drunk. It was like going to a Pogues concert except that Shane MacGowan was wearing seal fur instead of black denim. And there wasn't any Irish music. Or tin whistles. Actually, it wasn't like a Pogues concert at all. It was just pretty fucking sad. As there isn't a lot to do in Inuvik other than look at the one-sided trees, we had plenty of time to watch the drunken guys.

Concert day dawned cloudy and cold. With military precision, our planes took off one by one for the relatively short flight from Inuvik to Tuk, then cruised low over the Arctic tundra. Flat nothingness wherever the eye looked, like a slate of poorly endowed dancers at a bad strip club.

And then we landed in Tuktoyaktuk.

I don't ever want to hear you grouse about how there wasn't jack shit to do where you grew up unless you come from Tuk. The town itself was just a small collection of trailer-like homes, a few cinder-block buildings, and a couple of larger official structures. That was it. I managed to walk the entire burg in about ten minutes. The only thing of note was the very large, somewhat wolfish dogs tied up outside many of the domiciles. They each eyed me coolly, as if to say, "When the shit goes down up here, I'll eat you." It was my first, but not last, interaction in Canada's far northern regions with an animal who sized me up like an In-N-Out burger. It ain't no fun, but at least now I knew what the view looked like to Nina and Louise of Veruca Salt with an audience of guys leering at them.

All of the local people I met were great. They were as curious about we southerners as we were curious about them. Everybody was getting along great, taking pictures, shooting the shit, looking forward to the music. It further proved my belief that people are fine wherever you go. Yes, there are always some assholes, but for the most part people are pretty nice, especially when meeting strangers from distant lands.

At the edge of town was a large radar facility. Huge domes were set up as part of the Distant Early Warning detection system, aka The DEW Line, to monitor any incoming Russian nuclear missile attacks. This defense system had already been immortalized in the tune "Distant Early Warning" from the Canadian lads in the band Rush. We were warned that if we tried to approach it we'd be shot. A few people joked about trying to walk over, but I didn't. Call me old-fashioned, but I was brought up to believe that a man's skull is no place for a military policeman's bullet.

Speaking of cops, I found my buddy Constable Dave Dirksen. Seemed like a great guy with a sweet family. He said the other Mounties were looking forward to meeting me. Apparently, the tapes of Dave and I on the air together had become a hit in Arctic law enforcement circles, so I was greeted everywhere I walked like a celebrity. However, my offer to sing Frank Zappa's "Don't Eat The Yellow Snow" over the police radio was politely declined.

About the only thing the Mounties had to deal with was a small influx of uninvited Metallica fans. A handful of them, some from as far as Australia, chartered seaplanes that flew up and landed on the water at the edge of town. I was standing next to a group of the police when they asked Metallica's management what to do. The reply was, "They flew here in seaplanes? Fuck, that's great. Let 'em in!"

We then all gathered at the local school and were lined up in the cafeteria. Talk about a surreal rock and roll scene.

Every member of every band had lined up behind cafeteria tables and each one of us went down the line having an item autographed by all of them. As I was poorly prepared for this, I only had a blank piece of paper to get signed. After the show I stole some of the event posters off the wall and smuggled them back to the US. I've had most of the musicians from the concert sign them since then.

The only part that bummed me about this show was that there was no ticket stub. No one needed a ticket. If you were in Tuktoyaktuk, you were going to the show. Simple as that. Souvenirs from the trip would be in short supply.

Other than the fact that we were far enough north to hear Santa belch, it was like any other "meet and greet" I'd ever attended at a concert. The bands were pleasant but exhausted. One of the girls from Hole was very pale and shaking, and I doubted it had anything to do with the cold. We were being herded through at a pretty quick pace. All I managed to get, other than the signatures from the Metallica guys was from drummer Lars Ulrich, who looked up and said, "Hey, Lou. You made it. Fuck, I'm tired."

Speaking with Lars over the years, he would put this show in perspective with other historic Metallica gigs. When listing important shows he would mention the Arctic along with their five-nights at the Forum in LA, headlining Castle Donington, and their anniversary concerts at the Fillmore in San Francisco. He also brought up the Freddie Mercury tribute, the Guns N' Roses tour in '92, and the free show in Philly in '97. I'm glad to have attended many of those he mentioned.

From the school, we trooped over to the tent that was set up to house the show. Tent is an unfair word though. This thing looked like a flying saucer that had just touched down in a frozen trailer park. Inside was a large, low stage. A line of red-shirted security guards looked as grim and unfriendly as security guards I had seen at any other show I'd attended.

The event started with a bit of native dancing and a thank you from Mayor Eddie Dillon. The vibe was awesome. There was a feeling we were at something special. Something once in a lifetime. It was the kind of show that we all knew we could keep as our ace card when arguing with someone in future years at a bar about who had been to the coolest concert.

When later speaking to singer James Hetfield about seminal Metallica performances, he mentioned Tuktoyaktuk, Bonnaroo, and their second ever gig opening for Saxon at the Whisky. As much as he seemed to cherish those shows, I believe he's always looking for another live challenge.

Moist did a short, tight set. Veruca Salt was great. No, I didn't hit on them. Again, all that infatuation stuff was make-believe, even if it pissed my wife off for real.

It was during Hole's set that a wonderful thing happened. It's one of the coolest memories I have from the thousands of gigs I've attended. As the music blared and the crowd rocked, I stood in the middle of it all, slowly turning in a circle to take it all in. The music, the lights, the people, the smiles. The butterfly feeling in the pit of my stomach that I was standing on the very top of the world at an incredible event that would never come again. As I finished my circle, I came face-to-face with Metallica's singer James Hetfield, who was now standing in the crowd next to me with a beer in hand. He too was surveying the entire scene with a blissful look on his face. We must have realized that we were having the exact same thoughts. Neither of us said anything. We wouldn't have been able to hear one another over Courtney's clamoring anyway. We just looked at each other, smiled, and nodded with a look that said, "Can you fucking believe we're up here?" It was an awesome moment.

Finally, to the strains of Ennio Morricone's "The Ecstasy of Gold," Metallica took the stage. They opened with "Creeping Death" and did other favorites like "Master of Puppets," "Seek and Destroy," and "One." This was not a big, fancy arena show. How could it be? It was down and dirty Metallica, like the old days when I used to see them in bars so crowded you could lift your feet off the ground and allow the crowd to move you around.

The set was fourteen songs long, with the first encore being "Enter Sandman." To wrap the show, the band chose their cover of a tune that became a concert staple for them, the Anti-Nowhere League's "So What." Now I've heard all sorts of crazy songs. Some are funny. Some are stupid. Some are rude. But nothing beats "So What" for sheer, unadulterated offensiveness. It may be the greatest rock song ever recorded. No other tune can beat it for the sheer size of its lyrical balls.

A line from the opening verse summed up the entire Tuktoyaktuk experience rather nicely...

I've been here; I've been there
I've been every fucking where
So what, so what
So what, so what, you boring little cunt

As the song went on, I knew I had to get in the pit. I climbed up the back of the nearest person and began to crowd surf as Hetfield continued to spit out the lyrics...

And I've fucked a sheep; I've fucked a goat
I rammed my cock right down its throat
So what, so what
So what, so what, you boring little fuck

You have not lived a rock and roll life until you have crowd surfed with kids in polar bear fur at the top of the planet while listening to Metallica cover an English punk rock song with bestiality lyrics. It's a fucking fact.

Hearing "So What" was an epiphany. I would adopt it from that day forward as my on-air theme song in Chicago. I created a custom version with incredibly short beeps to cover as little of the more heinous lyrics as possible without setting off any FCC indecency alarms and played the shit out of it across the airwaves of Chicago.

On my last day on the air there, I played the song in its entirety. Unedited. Mike Fowler, the general manager of the station, was so pissed he didn't speak to me for a decade or two. Not that I can blame him *too* much.

Then in May of 2017, I was invited by the band to host their "Metallica: Now That We're Live" rehearsal special from Raven's Stadium in Baltimore. It was the group playing a few tunes for a small group of fan club members the night before the tour began. My job was to scurry around the stage, act as emcee, and do interviews with the band members. There were three hundred fans in attendance and millions watching online around the world.

As I was wrapping up on center stage at the end, Lars laughed and introduced me saying, "It's our new singer, Lou! Is there a particular Metallica song you want to sing?"

I'll give you one guess what I began to croon for the fans around the planet.

Certainly, the song is vile and disgusting, which should probably temper my love for it—but it hasn't. Call me old fashioned, but I was brought up to believe that a man's ear was the perfect place for goat fucking lyrics.

So fucking what
Yeah!

THE TIME SNOOP DOGG GOT ME SO HIGH
I DROOLED IN MY OWN LAP

IT WAS IN 2004 Linkin Park embarked on their third straight Projekt Revolution tour. The band did these jaunts to help illustrate and celebrate their belief in musical diversity. They had built their style and reputation on a hybrid of hard rock music and hip-hop and wished to put together concert lineups that reflected this aesthetic.

They began in 2002 playing indoor arenas for nineteen stops with a bill that included hip-hop pioneers Cypress Hill, nu-metal band Adema, and mash-up king DJ Z-Trip. The following year there were sixteen shows with an artist list featuring hard rockers Mudvayne (great fucking band!), rapper Xzibit, and Christian rockers Blindside.

However, it was this 2004 edition of Projekt Revolution where things really went off. The tour would play thirty-two amphitheaters from coast-to-coast with two stages and an incredible lineup. The main stage artists joining Linkin Park included nu-metal gods KoRn, hip-hop media maven Snoop Dogg, rockers The Used, and ska punkers Less Than Jake.

The tour began in Cincinnati on July 23. I wished to hit something fairly early in the proceedings so had my producer book interviews with the rockers on the tour at the gig in Camden, New Jersey, on Tuesday, August 3. It was this day that I was reminded why I don't do drugs.

The venue was the Tweeter Center at the Waterfront, one of the amphitheaters you see across the country, also known as "sheds." It's a big building with a ceiling covering the seating area, no walls, and a large lawn for cheaper general admission entrants. It's typical of these types of venues with the exception of its spectacular view of Center City Philadelphia, which was directly across the Delaware River.

At the time I had a townhouse in Annapolis, Maryland, which allowed easy access to my office and studios in Washington, DC. I planned on driving across the massive Annapolis Bay Bridge, over Chesapeake Bay, and then up the Eastern Shore, avoiding the nasty Route 95 corridor. It would take me about two hours each way on this sunny day, so I had a good vibe as I headed north with the windows down and the volume up.

I was feeling particularly good that morning. I was well rested as I'd recently returned from a vacation on the island of Bermuda. I'd brought back some Cohiba Mini Cuban cigars. These aren't big honking cigars, just the cigarette-sized ones you see Clint Eastwood chomping in the old spaghetti westerns. It was fun to smuggle them back, and it would be cool to walk around the show offering any friends on the tour real Cuban cigars. Though I didn't normally smoke them, I fired one up on the way to the gig.

I arrived at the venue, parked, picked up my credentials, and went about my business. I had interviews that day with

Linkin Park, KoRn, The Used, Funeral for A Friend, and Downset. Five interviews in half an afternoon sounds like a lot but, compared to a monstrosity like Rock on the Range, where I've done up to eighteen interviews in one day, this was a piece of cake. Everything ran like clockwork and the day went extra smooth as my producer, Roxy Myzal, was on site to help facilitate my appointments with the artists. At a festival tour like this, everyone is on a tight schedule, so things need to happen on time. An interview moving just five or ten minutes can be enough to totally fuck up your day by setting off a domino effect of missed appointments and angry tour managers calling you rude names. I know you think rock 'n' roll shows are supposed to be crazy and all, but people still gotta get their business shit done in a non-shitty businesslike way.

Anyway, it was late afternoon when I finished up my interviews and would finally be able to see some music performed. That's usually the biggest drawback of these huge festival shows: I often miss most of the music. I'm so busy running around doing press that there's no time to watch the actual concert. Yeah, I know, I know. You're crying a river of tears for me because my life of going to concerts is sooo hard. Fuck you.

I was checking the onstage schedule. KoRn was next on, and I wanted to take them up on their kind offer to sit in the soundboard area. However, producer Roxy walked up to me at that moment with a question. Would I be interested in talking to Snoop Dogg even though he wasn't on my original schedule? I have to be honest, even though I have what most people would consider a very large general knowledge of music, I'm pretty weak when it comes to hip-hop. I've got nothing against it, it just doesn't speak to my soul the way so much rock music does. However, I was very familiar with Snoop's cultural impact up to that point. He's an interesting guy. I didn't hesitate. "Yes, I'd love to speak with Snoop Dogg," I said.

One of the reasons I was keen to talk with him was that he had recently renounced the use of marijuana. Apparently, he was feeling like he was becoming too closely associated with drugs, particularly the weed from the devil's garden. I thought that was interesting ground to begin a conversation. Usually, I deeply research an artist before I speak with them, but this was going to be on the fly and I needed a place to start, so I assumed I'd lead with the weed thing.

Now then, let's take a quick detour to talk about drugs in general and weed specifically. I'll never go out of my way to tell you not to do anything. It's your life and if you wanna fuck it up, I suppose that's your business. However, if you ask for my advice, I'll tell you to stay away from any kind of drugs. I've had too many friends overdose or just burn themselves out from a wide array of chemical horseshit. Even if they don't flat out kill you, drugs will often rob you of your potential, as you're too busy being high to get anything done. There can also be nasty aftereffects. That's the main reason why I drink so little. The recovery time takes too long and I'd rather get up early and do cool shit instead of holding an icepack to my forehead. Please believe me when I say, if you wanna get wired, strong black coffee and loud music is the way to go. By the way, I realize caffeine is technically a drug, but you know what I mean. As for weed, I love the smell, but it makes me sleepy and paranoid. Then I fall asleep and have nightmares. However, I know many people who love the shit and at least they don't beat each other up the way drunks often do, so it can't be all that bad. I certainly believe that at the very least weed in its various incarnations should be available freely to those with debilitating medical conditions. Truly, if a cancer patient tells you weed eases their suffering, then they should be able to have all the fucking weed they want. It's just common sense, decency, and compassion.

These were the kinds of thoughts flitting through my brain as I walked toward the dressing room of the newly-clean-and-definitely-not-smoking-dope-anymore Snoop Dogg.

I knocked on his door and it opened just a crack. However, that was enough for a pressurized stream of Mary Jane smoke to escape as if it was steam shooting from Uncle Fester's ears in an original black and white episode of *The Addams Family*. I couldn't even see the face of whoever answered the door through the haze.

"Hey, I'm Lou. I'm here to see Snoop Dogg."

"Brutus, dog, git yer ass in here," came the reply from inside.

I was expected.

The door opened to a smoke-filled interior. It was like being on the side of Mount Fucking Doom in Mordor. I could barely see across the room. Even Cheech and Chong would have cried out "What da fuck?" at the sight of it. My tear ducts kicked into over drive as the clouds of concentrated cannabis accosted my corneas. I squinted as I looked up, and there was Snoop Dogg, a large parcel of friends behind him. I believe the word "posse" would be apropos under the circumstance. Snoop was tall and lean with a friendly smile as he held out his hand. I shook it and asked if we could set up on the nearby couch and coffee table.

You have to understand that through all this I'm thinking that Snoop Dogg no longer smokes. I had seen tons of articles and interviews and took them at their word. Even when the door opened to a cloud that seemingly floated in from some nineteenth-century impressionist painting, I assumed that Snoop's companions were hitting the pipe but that Snoop was clean.

I was wrong.

As I sat on the couch and put my small recorder and microphone down, I noticed a couple of cigars on the coffee table. Cigars? Of course! There's my conversational icebreaker! As Snoop obviously smoked cigars, I would offer him one of my Mini Cohibas from Cuba and set him at ease.

I took out the yellow and black box, opened it and pulled a cigar halfway out, offering it in Snoop's direction.

"Snoop, care for a Cuban cigar?

He beamed, "A Mini Cohiba? Brutus, you're a true pimp."

He took the cigar and smiled. I smiled too as I'd actually just been called a "true pimp" by Snoop Dogg himself. Not bad for a white boy from a New Jersey farm who grew up memorizing the lyrics to "Love Gun" from KISS.

I passed around the cigar box to the rest of the room and then settled in to do the interview. As I was just about to ask the first question, Snoop picked up one of his own cigars from the coffee table, lit it, and handed it to me with a small flourish.

"Gosh," I thought to myself, "Mr. Dogg is offering me one of his own cigars. What a pleasant chap!"

As I took it from his hand, I noticed a strange, pungent aroma rising from the cigar, an odor that didn't smell like tobacco of any kind. The strange scent piqued the interest of my olfactory perception as I looked down at the unlit end and noticed some sort of strange, green vegetation protruding out.

"That's odd," my still clueless inner voice said. "I certainly cannot recall any type of cigar-styled tobacco product that a featured a...OH MY GOD, IT'S MARIJUANA!!!"

Yup, it was a big ol' blunt. It started out its life as a normal cigar but had had the tobacco removed and replaced with weed. And by the smell of it, this wasn't any kind of regular dope that I'd ever encountered. This was some kind of nuclear-powered, Snoop Dogg-mutant-death weed that could probably wipe out an entire battalion of US marines with greater ease in a single hit than a neutron bomb.

What the fuck was I gonna do?!?!?! I hadn't been anywhere near weed in over a decade. The last time I'd had a hit off a joint was only because Hunter S. Thompson handed it to me and I didn't want to look like a douche by turning it down.

Snoop noticed my hesitation and looked at me strangely. Why was I just holding it? His guys also noticed so now everyone in the room was staring at me as I sat there with this giant hot stick in my hand.

I started to panic as sweat formed on my brow. "Jesus," I thought. "They're gonna figure me for a DEA narc and off me like it's some kinda deal gone wrong on *NYPD Blue*."

So I took a long hit off the blunt.

As my lungs relaxed, I exhaled a rainbow-colored cloud of kitties, puppies, and red-eyed smiley faces. A warm glow began to overtake my body and clear images of nachos, chocolate chip cookies, and other munchies formed in my brain.

Then I started coughing like a four-packs-a-day Lucky Strike smoker with my phlegm flying around the room.

"Yo, motherfucker. Cover your mouth," called out an annoyed Snoop.

Luckily, I was able to get the coughing down to a minimum before I gave myself an aneurysm. I was barely going to be able to function after just two pokes, but I managed to limp through the interview. Admittedly, most of the conversation consisted of me starting and stopping and forgetting what I was asking. My mind wandered during each of his answers and I came to the realization that I was really fucking high. What was in that blunt? I began to fear that it was laced with some fearful chemical and that's when the paranoia began to set in.

This is why I don't smoke weed.

We took a picture together. In it, Snoop is flashing some hand signs while I'm staring up at him with a grinning, red-eyed look of stupidity on my stoned face.

I thanked Snoop for his time, and fearful that I'd forgotten something in my crippled mental state, asked if I'd left any of my gear.

"No, man. You got all your shit. By the way, that's the fourth time you asked. You're all good."

I sensed it was time to leave and made my retreat.

By now I heard KoRn's set throbbing from the stage, so I stumbled out to the soundboard and took a seat on a large road case behind where their sound mixer stood. The music was loud but pleasant to my ears, and it felt good to be out of the dank cloud of dank. KoRn pounded out a succession of hits including "Falling Away from Me," "A.D.I.D.A.S.," and "Freak on a Leash." Meanwhile, I looked up at the ceiling of the venue and my vision began to get a bit fuzzy. The large bolts that held together the steel beams over my head slowly began to morph into different colors. As the hue changed, a ball of that color spun off the bolt to lazily float around the amphitheater. This continued until the air over my head was filled with a dizzying dance of colored balls floating in the hot summer evening.

What the fuck was in that blunt?

As I tried to bring myself back to a normal sense of consciousness, I felt a warm sensation in my thighs. As I turned my attention from the colorful ball dance over my head, I felt an itchy sensation on my chin. I then noticed a long, thick strand of drool from the corner of my mouth that stretched to a pool in my lap.

Holy shit, I was high.

Wait! Did I catch the sound man looking back and staring at me out of the corner of my eye, or was I just getting even more paranoid? Lord knows I must have looked like a heavily sedated extra from *One Flew Over the Cuckoo's Nest*.

The feeling of ill ease was only heightened by KoRn's music from the stage. The band had launched into their Pink Floyd cover song medley from "The Wall." The three movements of "Another Brick in the Wall" followed by the spirit-wrecking finale of "Goodbye, Cruel World" pushed me further into druggy delirium. I could not have heard the song's soul-crunching lyrics at a worse time.

As the fear rose in my brain, my breath came in short gasps, and that's when I came to the horrible realization that I had a two-hour drive ahead of me to get home.

Well, fuck me.

I went backstage and found Roxy for the first time since I'd left the dressing room, where she had continued to hit the Atomic Reefer of Blunty Death. She was sitting at a picnic table outside the catering area, going through the day's interviews and trying to add up segment times.

She cursed under her breath then drawled in a stoned voice, "Theeessse fucking times don't wanna add up right. This segment is sixteen minutes and forty seconds, and this one is twelve minutes and fifty seconds, which means they should add up to twenty-eight minutes and ninety seconds but the total is all fucked up."

"Roxy," I said, "there are sixty seconds in a minute—not a hundred."

"What? No, no, no. That's not it. It should be..." her voice trailed off incoherently.

It was time for me to leave.

The drive home was memorably horrible. I was so fucking skitzed out that I thought every car behind me was a cop preparing to pull me over. I also must have gone extra slow as the normal two-hour drive took nearly four. When I finally pulled into my driveway, I said a small prayer of thanks, went inside, ate three bags of potato chips, and passed out in my clothes on the floor, where I had paranoid dreams.

Dope: You Are What You Use.

THE TIME I ESCAPED THE WISCONSIN STATE POLICE AND THEIR FAKE PHALLUS FELONY ENFORCEMENT

IN 2005, RANDY HAWKE, program director for WJJO-FM in Madison, Wisconsin, told me that Slipknot was going to end their Subliminal Verses World Tour in town at the Alliant Energy Center. Randy and his station were among the first around the country to air my syndicated radio show, *hardDrive*, and I always looked forward to boozing and general stupidity with Randy and his staff. We arranged for me to fly in, surprise the band, and emcee the show.

First of all, a bit of background. I have a long history with the members of Slipknot going back to before their major label debut was released in 1999 on Roadrunner Records. I had received an advance of the release from Mark "Psycho" Abramson from the label of the still-as-yet-unmixed-album and fell in love with it. Without waiting for the rest of the world, I began playing the song "Wait and Bleed" before its release and raved about the band from coast-to-coast on my program. Unbeknownst to me at the time, Corey listened to the show every Sunday night on his hometown rock station in Des Moines, Iowa, KAZR-FM Lazer 103.3. In those days, he worked the night shift at a local porno palace. Corey later told me in our first interview together that he would tune in each week believing he would one day be a guest on the show. My feeling of pride at a future rock star being inspired by my program is, of course, naturally offset by the shame that said show provided the beat for beating off in the video booths of the shop. (More on my adventures with Corey and the other lads in "The Knot" elsewhere in this tome, hopefully without any references to public masturbatory habits. However, I make no promises.)

Corey and I are both big fans of the writer Hunter S. Thompson. In fits of stupidity, he and I often banter back and forth in Thompsonian voices with quotes from his books, like *Fear and Loathing in Las Vegas*. We screech about bats, leeches, and sexual intercourse with polar bears. We boast top-notch impressions of Thompson's voice and body mannerisms. Those around us think we're on serious medication, but that's their problem.

So, anyway, I thought it would be a splendid idea to show up dressed as Hunter S. Thompson. Thompson had taken his own life a couple of months before, and my costume was a goofy attempt to honor his memory. As I boarded my flight, I wore the full regalia of the late, hard-partying writer: high-top Chuck Taylors with athletic socks; brown cargo shorts; and a maroon, white, and blue Hawaiian shirt. The outfit was topped off by three key pieces: teardrop-shaped sunglasses, a red Dunhill cigarette in a holder, and a green plastic "Las Vegas" visor. Oh, one other thing, a flyswatter. Can't forget the flyswatter! It allows you to slap imaginary bats and smack people on various body parts.

A little background on the venue for the show, the Alliant Energy Center, formerly the Dane County Coliseum. It opened in 1967 and had a capacity of 10,231. Other notable shows there included Frank Sinatra, Elvis Presley, The Doors, Def Leppard, REO Speedwagon, KISS, and Cheap Trick.

As the cab dropped me off at the arena, the loading area was packed with tour buses and semi-trucks. Most of the buses were for Slipknot and their crew, but there were also vehicles for the other groups on the tour: Lamb of God and Shadows Fall. I always look forward to seeing Randy Blythe, lead singer of Lamb of God. He is also an author and accomplished photographer. He specializes in black-and-white photography using high-end Leica cameras. He often likes to photograph other photographers, calling it "Shooting the Shooters."

I wondered if Slipknot would keep to the time-honored tradition of the headlining band pranking the opening groups on the last night of a tour. The pranks could be anything from throwing rolls of toilet paper onstage to unplugging instruments to fucking with the lighting or sound systems. Tonight would set a new record for lurid creativity for tour-closing hijinks.

"Brutus!" I heard my name called out by crewmembers several times as I sauntered backstage. Among them was front of house sound man Dave "Shirt" Nicholls. "Shirt" was beloved by bands and fans alike for his incredible ears and ability to make even big, old, shitty arenas sound great for concerts. He was the preferred live sound mixer for both Slipknot and Avenged Sevenfold until his death from cancer in May of 2017.

Slipknot guitarist Mick Thomson was the first band member I *heard* coming. Mick's usual footwear is leather-studded jackboots, so his feet sound like marching storm troopers. He's well over six feet tall, which gives him an extra menacing look.

I was in the catering room attempting to pick up a slice of cheddar cheese with my flyswatter when I heard a voice yell from behind me, "SHIT! SHIT! SHIT!" It was Corey Taylor crying out in his Hunter S. Thompson voice to greet me. He let out a laugh as he surveyed my outfit. He was smoking from a Thompson-style cigarette holder, though that's where the gonzo similarities ended.

We went back to the dressing room, where we met up with Corey's wife at the time, Scarlett. Corey walked behind a curtain, and I assumed he was getting ready for his set. I offered to leave, but he insisted I stick around. While the three of us chatted, odd sounds emanated from behind the curtain. It sounded like the tearing of tape from a roll. It seemed to go on and on.

Finally, Corey said, "Okay, Hunter. I'm ready."

I turned around to face my friend, expecting him to be wearing a Slipknot jumpsuit. But he wasn't wearing a jumpsuit. He was wearing nothing on his body but a giant penis.

Made out of black duct tape and a plastic bag.

That hung down to near his knees.

My eyeballs rolled out of their sockets and bounced on the floor.

Egad! This was no normal phallus made of polyethylene, fabric mesh, and pressure sensitive adhesive. It was an elephant-sized Johnson bigger than the tusks of the famed Pyrrhus Pachyderms of the Old World.

A schlong so huge it needed its own zip code.

A weenie longer than the guitar solo from "Do You Feel Like We Do" on *Frampton Comes Alive*.

It was one big mutha-fuckin' dick.

As I picked my jaw up off the cement and used it to corral my eyeballs back into place, I took a gander at Corey from head to toe. His shoulder-length hair was pulled into two pigtails. His current Slipknot mask covered his face like a second skin of singed flesh. He wore nothing else but an evil grin.

Well, nothing besides the Louisville Slugger–sized simulated schwanz waving back and forth between his knees.

I don't know how it was all held together. Maybe he wrapped his cock in a sock first. It's a mystery best left unsolved.

Corey leered at me and said, "Let's go."

I thought, "*Go? Go where?*"

He put on a gold robe as he walked to the dressing room door, then pressed down on the duct-tape dong to keep it under the folds of the robe and picked up a drumhead that contained some kind of messaging from the floor. Scarlett gave me a small push from behind to get my feet moving. Corey was a man on a mission. He walked quickly and deliberately through the backstage hallways, ignoring the stares, points, and giggles from the crew and fans backstage. I quickly realized we weren't heading to catering, the production office, or the buses.

We were on our way to the stage.

You should know that everywhere backstage at big venues are neon arrows of tape on the floor pointing you toward important places like catering, the stage, or the dressing room. If you don't know where to go, look at the floor! The Rev from Avenged Sevenfold once joked to me, "If those arrows pointed to a cliff, I'd walk right off!" We seemed to be following the tape that pointed to the stage.

As we traipsed along, it hit me. This would be one of the greatest tour-ending pranks of all time! I chuckled as I pictured the faces of the Shadows Fall guys when they realized they were sharing the stage with a sticky gray tallywhacker of ginormous proportion.

The stage was crammed with the equipment of the three bands playing that night. Shadows Fall were soldiering through their set, oblivious to the penile indignity that was mere seconds away.

Scarlett and I stopped on the edge of stage.

Corey kept going.

Shadows Fall (SHADS for short) is a great band. Originally from Springfield, Massachusetts, Phil Labonte of All That Remains was vocalist before Brian Fair joined up in 1999. They are two-time Grammy nominees for Metal Performance for the songs "What Drives the Weak" in 2006 and "Redemption" in 2008. The band has toured the world and seen most everything touring musicians can see. But they had never witnessed anything like this.

Corey Taylor walked to the center of the stage in the middle of a song and parted his robe, holding his arms straight out. He held the pose for just a moment, much like Buffalo Bill preening for the video cam in *Silence of the Lambs*. Unlike Bill, he did not tuck his manhood away.

The giant duct-tape penis waved out in the open for all to see.

Wisconsinites love bratwurst, but they had never seen a sausage as large and fierce as the one waving across the arena stage though this one admittedly used non-meat filler.

The roar of the audience drowned out the intense volume of Shadows Fall as Corey dropped his robe and pranced about the stage in between the band members, his pigtails bouncing up and down to the beat of the music while his wondrous wang waved at a slightly slower speed.

Corey now raised the drumhead over his head triumphantly. It read "I ♥ SHADOWS FALL."

The eyeballs of the SHADS lads rolled out of their sockets and bounced on the floor. However, as they're total pros, nobody missed a note.

It was then that I heard Scarlett's voice behind me: "You're on, Hunter."

She shoved me hard onto the stage toward Corey.

Time seemed to slow down as I stumbled across the stage trying to regain my balance. The sound of the music and the roar of the crowd melted away while the lights seemed to get brighter and I felt their heat on my face.

For a moment, I thought I felt the squish of a Shadows Fall eyeball underneath the sole of my sneaker.

It was then that my Hunter S. Thompson outfit–inspired reflexes kicked in. I began chasing Corey around the stage, waving at his Dong of Doom with my flyswatter.

I don't know how long this went on. More than likely just a few seconds, though it seemed like a few minutes. Twenty thousand eyes fixed upon the musicians, flyswatter, and duct-tape trouser trout moving in an insane rock 'n' roll ballet. I took a few swipes at the SHADS members then moved in to deliver a coup de grâce and claim victory over the imitation baloney pony before escaping to the dressing room. Unfortunately, I miscalculated Corey's next move. He doubled back as I raised my wrist above my head and

I narrowly missed being slapped across the face by his sticky ersatz schnitzel.

There are a lot of humiliating things that can happen if you choose a life in rock 'n' roll radio. You could screw up on the air. You could be publicly fired. However, you won't know true humiliation until you've almost been smacked upside the kisser by another man's fake flesh flute in front of ten thousand screaming metal heads.

The first thought that came to mind in this pre-smart phone time in history was how lucky I was that no one would ever see this moment of my life.

I was wrong.

As I looked into the pit before the stage, I came eye to eye with the lens of a professional grade camera.

"Click-click-click" went the shutter.

"Shit-shit-shit" went the voice in my head.

The photographer turned out to be the great Chad Lee. Yes, the images still exist. No, you don't want to see them.

While I did escape the chafe from of the chubby on my cheek, I'd wrenched my knee on the floor, and the pain reminded me to retreat to the far side of the stage. Corey went back to the side we had come from.

My exit wasn't as uneventful. I ran (with a slight limp) into two displeased Wisconsin state troopers. I've had to explain a lot of crazy shit in my career, but I had no intention of giving a demented dick dissertation to a couple of pissed off John Laws. So I took the manly way out.

I fucking ran for it.

My heels moved so quickly they kicked up sparks. I pictured some deputy district attorney drooling at the thought of bringing headline-grabbing charges like "Unlawful

Possession of a Phony Pork Sword" or "Illegal Discharge of a Fallacious Love Gun" against me and Corey. I had no desire to find out what the penalties (penal-ties?) would be.

I made my way toward the luxury box reserved for WJJO, doing my best to avoid anyone in uniform. I changed into a Slipknot concert T-shirt and darted between concertgoers in the hallway, ditching my glasses, cigarette holder, and green visor in the large pockets of my cargo shorts.

Yes, as I mentioned earlier, I had cargo shorts on. It was part of my Hunter costume. Please don't make fashion fun of me about it, as the rest of this chapter should be embarrassing enough as it is.

Bursting through the door of the radio station's suite, I saw Randy Hawke and WJJO promotions director Bonnie Oleson, among others. Before they could quiz me about the onstage stupidity, I cried out at the top of my lungs, "I'm not here!"

Then I locked myself in the bathroom where I noticed my now slightly bloody knee beginning to swell up.

Naturally, I missed the rest of the set from Shadows Fall as well as most of music from Lamb of God. It was especially tough not seeing Lamb of God. I really wanted to catch the set, but not so much that I was willing to risk being pimped out for a pack of smokes in lockup that night.

In the meantime, the angry denizens of the luxury box banged on the door of the bathroom as they suffered the pain from their beer-swollen bladders. I felt bad for them, but not bad enough to risk possible arrest. Only the need to return to the stage—to do my short emcee duties shortly before Slipknot—brought me out of the john.

How intent the coppers were on finding the culprits is unknown. I vectored around anyone with a badge as

I returned to the stage, hoping I was safe without the Hunter S. Thompson getup. I gave the quickest stage announcement in history.

"I'M LOUBRUTUSFROMTHEWORLDFA-MOUSHARDDRIVEONNINTYFOURONEWJJOAND-SLIPKNOTWILLBEUPINJUSTAMOMENT!"

I was going to exit the building soon after my second visit to the limelight, but then Slipknot hit the stage. Their set began with the searing "The Blister Exists." It was during the second song, "Sic," that Shadows Fall attempted a bit of payback in the prank department.

While hiding on the side of the stage, the SHADS members placed a large, yellow, radio-controlled dump truck on the floor and sent it onto the stage. It was a nice try at a bit of fun, but it did not take into account the fact that there were nine fucking lunatics flailing about onstage.

After the dump truck got a few feet out, percussionist M. Shawn Crahan ("Clown") hit it with his aluminum baseball bat. Chris Fehn ("Long Nose"), the other percussionist, joined in with a large metal pipe. In mere seconds, the dump truck was beaten to pieces.

One of the larger truck parts skidded to where I was standing, and I picked it up as a souvenir. I later had Shawn and Chris autograph it. I don't remember if it's buried someplace in the crates of memorabilia I've collected through the years or if I gave it to WJJO for a charity auction.

Which brings me to an important tip: SAVE EVERYTHING! Passes, ticket stubs, wristbands, and anything else related to a rock show are collectible. Throw nothing away! If it's not readily identifiable, add a small piece of masking tape with a note stating what it's from. Anything from the stage is extra collectible. Well, except thrown water bottles. I don't know anyone who collects rock star backwash. However, as I once scooped up fake wig hair trimmed from the head of Tobias Forge of Ghost, I'm the last one who will point fingers at anyone collecting anything.

Sadly, my night was about over as I saw the Wisconsin state troopers eyeing me inquisitively. I darted offstage, out the back door, and into a cab.

While there were fortunately no physical scars from dodging the duct-tape weenie, I will carry the emotional scars forever.

THE TIME DR. HUNTER S. THOMPSON MENACED ME WITH DEPRAVED VIOLENCE AND A BOTTLE OF CHIVAS REGAL

As you've probably figured out from the previous chapter, I'm a big fan of Hunter S. Thompson and have been since I was a kid. Some people look up to athletes, statesmen, or religious figures. I idolized a seemingly drugged-out writer with a cigarette holder. Don't judge me. When I arrived at WHJY in Providence, Rhode Island, in 1988, I began closing my show with a quote from one of Hunter's books. It was that same year that he published his book *Gonzo Papers, Vol. 2: Generation of Swine: Tales of Shame and Degradation in the '80s.*

His promotion of that book would put us on a collision course that would rank among the most exhilarating in my strange little life.

Late in '88, I received a call on the studio request line from a man named Stanky who identified himself as an agent of Summit Books, the then current publisher of Thompson's work. He was based in Boston but his work regularly brought him to Providence, where he tuned in to my show and often heard the on-air Thompson quotes. Hunter would soon be making a live appearance at the Somerville Theatre in Somerville, Massachusetts. It was near Harvard University in Cambridge, wedged between the Charles and Mystic Rivers, part of the Boston metropolis. Stanky had made the call to invite me to the show to meet Hunter.

My heart leapt to my throat as visions of Thompson's violent, drug-addled behavior danced through my head. Would he truly turn out to be like the characterizations of himself in his books? Would he walk onstage snorting cocaine off the barrel of an AK-47? Was it possible he'd pull a pair of pearl-handled revolvers from beneath his jacket and empty the chambers into the air while slamming a bottle of Wild Turkey?

There was only one way to find out.

On first learning of Hunter's appearance, I immediately notified one of the other radio-station DJs, Rick O'Brien, *aka* Rick O. B., or simply OB. He was another dedicated fan of Hunter's, and we began to plan for a debauched evening of literary excess. There would be an early and a late session from Thompson that night, and we hoped to stay for both.

The scheme called for us to be taken to Boston in a limousine, as we figured the percentile chance of intoxication by us both was actually well beyond one hundred percent. The limo would have to be stocked with an eye on the possibility that we could end up partying with Hunter in person. It was like preparing the logistics for an invasion by a division of marines whose main objective was to kill the enemy by getting them inhumanly fucked-up. We purchased over a dozen bottles of hard liquor, several cases of beer, and a case of grapefruit (a nod to Thompson's grapefruit reference in *Fear and Loathing in Las Vegas*). Rick also acquired some weed in anticipation that we might spark up with Thompson.

However, it was not garden-variety grass, for how could we offer such an illustrious connoisseur of drugs common dirt leaf? It was some kind of superbly special smoke, guaranteed to make the user comatose with just one hit.

The evening of the show arrived with OB and I happily ensconced in the back of our limousine, rocketing northbound up I-95 for the hour-and-a-half-long ride. I swilled Jack Daniels straight from the bottle as Rick hacked grapefruit to pieces with a giant hunting knife and the Neil Young scored soundtrack from the Hunter Thompson–inspired film *Where the Buffalo Roam* roared from the speakers. We yelled above it to trade quotes from Thompson's books as our brains became fully lubricated by the copious amounts of alcohol we swilled as if Charles Bukowski had somehow anointed our livers with superpowers for this special night.

"We must now smoke the good smoke, Brutus, old chum," said OB. His eyes were glazed over in a way that caused me no small worry.

"Don't be a fool," I implored. "If we tangle with that wretched plant now, the stench of it will be taken on the sniff by every Massachusetts State Trooper from here to Fenway Park. Are you ready to be someone's wife at the Suffolk County Jail? I'm not. My hindquarters get sore just thinking about it."

Though we successfully fought the urge to light up, we still felt no pain as we poured from the car when it pulled up to the grand old Somerville Theatre. Originally opened in 1914, the Somerville was built as an all-purpose venue that featured vaudeville acts, opera, and plays. It later added motion pictures, folk music, and rock bands as the decades rolled on. It's a phenomenal place where you can feel the history dripping from the walls. Still in operation to this day, it seats about eight hundred people who pass underneath an old-fashioned marquee to walk through its front doors. For me and OB, the walk was more of a crawl.

"How are you feeling?" Rick asked.

"I don't *feel* anything," I said. "I'm pretty numb from the forehead down. I may wind up incontinent. Please have the good sense to shove me in the direction of the gents' room if you see any wet spots forming in my jeans."

I feared we would never find Stanky in the circus-like crowd of Thompson fans that swelled the lobby of the theatre. The vaudevillians of days gone by had never seen a group like this, many in T-shirts featuring the nightmarish art of Thompson book illustrator Ralph Steadman, others dressed in costume as Hunter himself. Almost all drained glasses of one alcoholic concoction or another while some were seen to snort white powder from small, brown vials. A few had the tell-tale psychedelic gleam indicating that their evening was being brought to them by the letters L, S, and D.

I was disappointed not to see any giant bats screeching through the air of the lobby.

A voice called above the din of the crowd, "Brutus, there you are!" It was Stanky. "Come with me now," he pleaded and threaded us quickly through the lobby, into the main theatre, around to a backstage area, and then to a door. "The doctor isn't in yet, but he'll be here soon enough. We must prepare for him."

Stanky led us through the door and down the scariest staircase I had ever encountered in my life. It was barely wide enough for me to walk down without my shoulders scraping the walls. The steps themselves were so steep it almost felt like walking forward down a ladder. Add to that the loss of motor coordination that normally comes with the imbibing of a half-bottle of Tennessee sour mash and you'll understand why I felt acidic bile rising from my innards.

"Thank God you're walking in front of me, Stanky. You'll break my fall if I go over headfirst." He chuckled a bit until I said, "Why are you laughing? I'm not kidding." OB latched onto my shoulder from behind to steady us both.

The bottom step emptied directly into the Somerville's dressing room. It was right beneath the stage and could probably fit about ten people comfortably. There was easily twice that inside. Most of them stood crowded together, a lucky few sat on a small couch in the middle of the room, and others surrounded a small card table off to the right that had been set up as makeshift bar. About half a dozen bottles of booze were being sampled by those who could find space to bend their elbows and raise their glasses. There was one door, slightly ajar, that went into a small bathroom. Each set of eyes looked up expectantly as we walked down and into the room only to turn away disappointedly when realizing none of us was the man himself.

I stopped and stood at the foot of the steps, as there wasn't much room to go anywhere else.

Stanky now whispered to me conspiratorially, "Hunter should be arriving any minute. Make yourselves comfortable, if that's possible in here. When he comes down, don't make any sudden moves toward him as he may not react well."

I wondered what the term "not react well" could encompass.

I would soon find out as the door at the top of the staircase opened. The sound of the expectant dressing room mob, now grown agitated with delay, filtered down until the door closed again. Heavy, uneven footsteps came closer down the staircase.

Then there was stumbling on the narrow steps, a guttural shout, and a body tumbled onto the floor next to me.

Everyone in the room froze and went silent like a herd of wildebeest that had just seen a cheetah in a pair of Ray Bans fall out of a nearby tree.

It was Hunter S. Thompson.

He was down on his hands and knees, cursing under his breath. His well-chewed cigarette holder, a smoldering Dunhill still lit inside of it, on the floor beneath him. I steadied his arm as he picked himself up, wedged his cigarette holder back between his teeth, and dusted himself off. We then stood face-to-face.

Hunter Thompson was tall. Taller than I had imagined he would be, standing half a head higher than me. His complexion told of a life spent outdoors in fresh mountain air and away from dark bars, regardless of his tales of debauchery. He had the physical build of a man of action and movement. He wore a windbreaker, blue Polo by Ralph Lauren shirt with red logo, a baseball cap, and amber shades.

I held out my hand to shake his and began to introduce myself.

"Hello, Dr. Thompson. It's a pleasure to me you. My name is...GAAAHHHHH!!!"

Hunter shoved his left forearm under my chin and into my neck. He jacked me up against the wall, where I had to stay on the tips of my toes to keep from being choked. Through the tint of his shades, I saw that the pupils in his eyes were as big as ostrich eggs. His breath stank of booze, cigarettes, and madness. He shouted at me through clenched teeth that caused his cigarette holder to jut straight up toward the plastered ceiling.

"WHO THE FUCK ARE YOU?!?! WHAT THE FUCK DO YOU WANT?!?!"

His voice quivered with rage. I tried to speak but couldn't, as he had worked his elbow up near my Adam's apple. I looked at him in terror, the blood draining from my face and the air from my lungs. My eyes darted downward to see his right hand reach into his windbreaker pocket and take out what looked to be an umbrella handle. His thumb hovered over its small release button.

My fading consciousness wondered, "What the hell is he doing with an umbrella?"

In a last, desperate attempt to forestall my untimely demise, I wrenched sideways and managed to hiss a few words from my air-deprived lungs.

"Doc, my name is Brutus. I'm here with Stanky. I'm a friend."

His left arm now eased a bit on my neck and I was able to stand flat-footed. My breath came in gasps but at least now I didn't feel I was going to black out. His right hand still held the umbrella handle close to my chest.

I steadied myself and continued, "It's nice to meet you. I've read all your work." I held out my hand again to shake his, leaning in a bit, my chest almost touching the umbrella.

The tenseness left his body as he stood back and returned the umbrella to his pocket. "Your name is Brutus," he said. It was a statement, not a question.

I nodded my head and forced a smile. Hunter grasped my proffered hand and used it to again pull me close. We were almost cheek to cheek.

"Brutus. You're a man. You are brave. You and I are brothers!"

Quick as a cat, Thompson spun around and put his arm over my shoulder, squeezing me in a crushing embrace as he shouted to the still, shell-shocked room.

"THIS IS BRUTUS. HE IS A FUCKING WARRIOR. HE'S HERE WITH ME. FUCK WITH HIM AT YOUR OWN PERIL!!!"

His voice dropped back down as he turned to me, "Do you drink? Of course you drink! We must drink together like men!"

Keeping me wrapped with his right arm, Hunter shoved past some still stunned onlookers, led me to the card table bar, and grabbed an open bottle of Chivas Regal whisky. His right hand reached up and pulled the hair on the top of my head to wrench it back to face the ceiling.

"Drink. Drink it, it's good for you," he cackled as the nearly full bottle poured both into my mouth and across my face. "Don't be a fucking baby. Take your medicine."

I managed to down it without gagging. He let go of my hair and spoke to me as I wiped the scotch from me face.

"You're with me, Brutus! We're friends now. I must meet these other swine, but you and I shall drink again in a moment."

He then turned and began, in a somewhat more benign style, to speak with the others in the room. After a few minutes, relative calm returned but for the blurted expletives from Thompson, who was working the room much in the way I had expected he would, like a barely controlled crazy person.

Stanky did many of the introductions. Some of those in the room held out books to be signed, a few asked for pictures. At one point, Thompson and he whispered to one another and looked in my direction. Hunter pointed the gnawed end of his cigarette holder at me and nodded approvingly.

When OB was introduced to Hunter, he pulled out his long-held joint of zombie death leaf. Hunter lit it and ordered me to partake. Normally, I never touched the stuff, but who was I to turn down the medicinal advice of a doctor? The three of us then took a snapshot together with a wild-eyed girl, the brain-draining stick of weed dangling from the corner of OB's mouth in the picture.

A few minutes later, Stanky sidled over to speak to me with a look of awe on his face.

"Jesus, I've never seen the Doctor take to someone like that before. He really likes you. It's pretty fucking amazing. At first, I thought you were a goner."

"Yeah, I was scared shitless but then things turned right around," I said.

Stanky huffed a bit as he continued, "C'mon, dude. Don't be so modest. The guy held a fucking cattle prod an inch from your chest and you didn't even flinch. Shit, you actually leaned toward it at one point."

I could feel the color drain from my face. "Cattle prod? What the fuck are you talking about? I thought he had an umbrella in his hand."

"Christ Almighty," he said. "He'd have knocked you through the wall with that thing. You'd be in an ambulance on the way to Mass General right now if he had hit your chest and pressed that button."

"No wonder he called me a warrior," I offered meekly.

"He thinks you have balls made of pure fucking steel. Don't say anything more about it as it could change his mood and I've gotta get him out there for the early show," he said looking at his watch, which read long past the announced start time.

The show itself consisted of Thompson sitting on a couch at the center of the ill-lit stage, taking questions from the audience who spoke into microphones set up in the aisles.

I actually got to ask the first question: "Dr. Thompson, if you were given..."

"I CAN'T SEE YOU OUT IN THE DARK!!!" he yelled.

Hunter sprang to his feet and ran offstage, only to return a few seconds later with a large flashlight in his hand, which he side-armed into the audience in my general direction. I retrieved it from the floor, shined the light up into my face and continued.

"Dr. Thompson, if you were given your choice of any kitchen utensil to shove up Garry Trudeau's ass, what would it be?" It was a reference to his professed hatred of the creator of the Doonesbury comic strip, who based the character Uncle Duke in it on Hunter's likeness and demeanor.

"You're a very sick young man," he replied. In the dark, I couldn't see whether or not he smiled as he said it.

The Q&A went about an hour before ending for a set break, which would allow the audiences to change over. When OB and I returned to the dressing room, the mood had turned foul.

Stanky looked at me with a worried face and gestured at the now closed door to the dressing room bathroom. A few seconds later fists pounded against it from within and a voice bellowed.

"NO BLOW! NO SECOND SHOW! NO BLOW! NO SECOND SHOW!"

"He wants cocaine," Stanky said in a panicked voice. "He wants cocaine or he's not going out to do the late show."

"NO BLOW! NO SECOND SHOW! GET ME SOME FUCKING COKE OR I SWEAR I'LL KILL ALL OF YOU!"

"What the fuck am I supposed to do?" Stanky asked despondently.

Someone else in the room pointed at OB and I. "Those guys have a limo parked out front. They could get in and out quickly. I know a place to score from close by in Cambridge. I'll give them the address and they can be back in a few minutes."

The guy whipped out a wad of bills that foretold an amount of coke so big that we'd need Sherpa guides from Nepal to carry it all back. OB and I exchanged worried glances. We had come up to have fun, not act as drug mules for an exchange that could land us both in a federal pen on trafficking charges.

Yeah, I know. When it came time to go over the edge in a real life showing of Thompson's gonzo lifestyle, we pussied right the fuck out.

"Ahhhhh, sorry. We gotta bolt. It'll take hours to get back to where we're from." OB and I scrambled up the stairs, using both hands and feet to scale the awkward steps quickly. We passed into the theatre and outside to where our driver waited.

"I thought you guys were going to be later than this," the driver said. "Do you want to leave now?"

"We want to leave fast," was our reply.

OB and I said little on the way back. I think we were both emotionally and physically exhausted by our brief time with Hunter. The booze and dope had also taken their toll. We both passed out on the ride back to Providence.

The car dropped OB off first. "That was a hell of a thing," he smiled. "Too bad we didn't have a chance to get our books signed."

"No matter," I replied. "We passed through the belly of the beast and right out its rectum. That was a night for the ages."

While Rick and I talked about our adventure on the air, we left out some of the more incriminating details. It was several months later that I was answering the request lines when I heard the familiar voice of Stanky on the other end.

"Hunter's coming back," he said. An invitation was extended. "You need to come and meet him again. I told him about how you close your show with a quote from his books and that you actually understand what he's writing about."

OB and I arrived that night by limousine again but with far less bluster. I think we both wanted to have our wits about us if things got weird. We were careful to walk down the steps safely into the dressing room and were pleased to see a far smaller group there this time. We actually got to sit on the couch and arranged the books we had brought on the table in front of us. On the drive up, we had discussed how there was absolutely no chance Hunter would remember us from our previous meeting.

Thompson walked in a few minutes later. He waved his arms around his head and yelled as he entered. On seeing OB and I, he stopped cold. He looked me directly in the eyes, stared mutely for a moment, but then spoke.

"Brutus. Great to see you again. Sorry about the cattle prod. It was uncalled for. I'm ashamed. Forgive me."

He then turned to OB, saying, "Ahhh, Rick. Your name is Rick but they call you OB, You are the keeper of the good smoke."

He looked at Stanky and raged, "All right! Get everyone the fuck out of here! I want them all out! I wanna talk to my friends, goddamnit!" He gestured at Rick and I, much to our delight.

Hunter's back was still turned to us as the last person went up the steps. When they were gone, his shoulders noticeably drooped. He let out a deep breath and turned around. His gonzo demeanor seemed to be melting away. He walked over to the couch and sat down with us.

"Nice to see you again. Sorry about all the stupid shit. Part of the job."

The crazy man was now completely gone. It was as if a Mr. Hyde to Dr. Jekyll transformation had taken place right before our eyes. The fellow who sat in with us was a soft-spoken Southern gentleman. Neither Rick nor I said a word as he continued.

"Brutus, they told me how you use the quotes on your show and that you actually understand what it all means. It's not all about drugs and stupidity. It's about America and about truth. Anyway, I appreciate it."

He turned to Rick, saying, "You too, Rick. You get it. I appreciated how you guys handled yourselves last time. Things go a bit off for me sometimes."

We then made small talk. I don't honestly remember much of the conversation. I think it was probably about music and bands that he liked. After a few minutes, he found a scrap of paper, wrote out a phone number on it, and shoved it into my hand.

"This is my kitchen number. Call me anytime. Well, just don't call when the sun is still up," he said with a grin.

He then looked at our copies of his books on the table, which he graciously offered to sign. We accepted gratefully.

As he handed the last one back, he said, "Listen, I gotta let these people back in again. I just wanted to take a few moments to say thank you like a human fucking being."

With that he got up, walked back to the staircase, and shouted, "ALL RIGHT, YOU MOTHERFUCKERS, GET BACK DOWN HERE!"

Rick and I exchanged a glance. What had just transpired was more shocking than the booze, drugs, and cattle prods of our previous meeting. We had actually met the real Hunter S. Thompson.

The rest of the night passed uneventfully. I had Stanky autograph page 283 where he's mentioned in *Generation of*

Swine. We then went up and watched the show, but it didn't have the fire of the previous one we had seen. The format of the show this time called for Hunter to be joined by several Boston-area media personalities, but it quickly turned chaotic and uninformative. OB and I left before it was over.

I never did meet Hunter again in person, although I often took him up on his offer to phone his kitchen hotline. I usually rang him late at night when I had a buzz on and wished to get his take on something happening in the political arena. He was always awake and willing to talk.

One winter several years later, I was in Vail, Colorado, to accompany some contest winners. I was going to grab a car and drive through the mountains to where Hunter lived outside of Aspen. I wasn't sure whether I'd have the nerve to go all the way up to his "fortified compound" of Owl Farm unannounced. I'd at least get to his favorite watering hole Woody Creek Tavern nearby, where I could call and invite him out for a drink. However, snow and ice came in and closed down the mountain passes, so I was unable to attempt the journey.

The last time we spoke was in 2003. I wanted to see if he was interested in hosting a show on XM Satellite Radio and let him know that the set up of the program could be anything of his choosing. He could talk politics and social issues with absolutely no restraint on language or content. Likewise, he could host a music show where he chose every piece of music. If he wanted to do a combination of both, he could do both.

Sadly, he passed, saying, "I just don't see it. It might be fun for a time or two but then I'd get bored and would stop doing it. The last thing I need is more deadlines to miss."

When it was announced that he had shot and killed himself, I took it hard. I'm sure I would have taken it poorly even if I had never met him, but what made it tougher were those few minutes of soft-spoken conversation he had with Rick OB and myself. I keep his kitchen number on my cell phone to this day.

Hunter's funeral was a grand affair. A ton of stars that had befriended him through the years gave him a crazy send-off about six months after he died. Lyle Lovett, Sean Penn, and others watched as Hunter's cremated remains were shot into the sky by a giant cannon to explode in the night over a 150-foot tower raised in his honor. I thought of attending with the rest of the uninvited public but just didn't have the heart.

The cannon and much of the costs were paid for by Thompson's friend Johnny Depp, who famously portrayed Hunter in the film adaptation of *Fear and Loathing in Las Vegas*. I've never met Johnny Depp. However, if I do, I'd like to hand him a hundred-dollar bill and say the following:

"Mr. Depp, you don't know me. I'm a fan of your late friend Dr. Hunter S. Thompson. I know you don't need the money, but it would make me feel good if you would accept this as my share of the costs for his cannon send-off. I hope you'll use it to do something unusual that would have made Hunter happy. Thanks for what you did."

Now please understand that I don't claim to have been an intimate of Hunter's, nor am I suggesting that we were friends. I barely knew the guy. However, I can proudly say that, once upon a time, the world's greatest writer held an electric cattle prod to my chest and poured whiskey down my throat.

And that's good enough for me.

THE TIME MOTLEY CRUE'S ROADIES SHOWED ME THE GROSSEST THING IN THE HISTORY OF WESTERN CIVILIZATION

IT WAS ON FRIDAY the thirteenth of April 1990 in Providence, Rhode Island, that I had the accursed luck to be shown the grossest thing in the history of Western Civilization. The memory of it gives me the dry heaves to this day.

Mötley Crüe was touring behind their opus *Dr. Feelgood* and was in town at the Providence Civic Center for two sold-out shows. Opening the concerts would be Faster Pussycat, a glam metal band out of Los Angeles named for the Russ Meyer exploitation film *Faster, Pussycat! Kill! Kill!*

Little did I know that the first of these two evenings would leave one of the most disturbing images created by the Hand of Fallen Man etched onto my retinas for the rest of eternity, while the second would place me in the pantheon of those sub-humans who turn such images into song.

I had seen the Crüe a bunch of times before, but the buzz on this show was epic. This was an already legendary band at the zenith of their powers and popularity. The shows were part of a two-year tour behind a platinum selling album, with an elaborate stage show that featured a flying drum kit, rising piano, and (very) long-legged back-up singers dressed like nurses, as well as enough pyrotechnics to make the stage light up like the candles on Methuselah's birthday cake.

My kinda show.

At this time, I was doing the afternoon drive program at radio station WHJY-FM. It was the big rock station in Southern New England. As such, I was given the honor of emceeing the concerts. This sounds like a lot of fun, and it was, but being the radio guy onstage at one of these things is also in many ways one of the most unglamorous duties in music.

That's because a radio DJ is considered by many to be the lowest rung of the entertainment world ladder. Well, perhaps one notch above a clown at children's parties, but that's about it. Actually, if the clown is really good with balloon animals, the radio DJ falls back to the bottom.

After getting off the air that evening, I headed across town to the Civic Center. There was a ticket waiting for me along with a backstage pass. However, this wasn't an ordinary cloth pass with sticky backing, it was a laminated All-Access pass. My head swelled several hat sizes at the sight of it. I rated a laminate! It would allow me god-like powers for the night. I could come and go as I please. I could march unhindered backstage to use private bathrooms whose tiles were not a furry blanket of pubes that fell from the masses of quickly zipped crotches in the public john. I could casually slip the pass into my shirt pocket in a show of false modesty when running into friends and coworkers but not until after I had made absolutely sure that they had seen it first. I still have that pass today.

My chest puffed out an extra six inches to allow people walking by me a better look at the pass; I strutted backstage to the production office. This is the nerve center of a big arena-sized show. It's usually a few folding tables used as desks with offstage personnel handling the business of the tour. Phones ring. People sometimes yell. It is not often a happy place. The folks to be found there are usually overworked, under-rested, and don't have a lot of patience for the nightly chore of dealing with the man or woman who represents the lowest rung of the entertainment ladder in that market.

However, on this night I wasn't concerned about that. All-Access pass in plain sight, I confidently strode up to the nearest desk and exclaimed, "I'm Lou Brutus. I'm hosting the show tonight." A disinterested woman covered in bizarre tattooed images of the Orient looked up and asked, "How the fuck did you get a laminate?" I replied, "It's, uhhhh. I'm Lou and, um-mmmm." My voice trailed off and the cocky cockiness melted away. "They shouldn't have given you a laminate. You should have these cloth passes," she said as she shoved them into my hand. "You can keep the lam, but if you try to walk into the dressing rooms, I'll personally beat the living shit out of you."

I was pretty sure she would and could do it.

I was told that I'd take the stage exactly ten minutes after the end of Faster Pussycat's set, which would allow the road crew time to remove their gear from the stage—Mötley Crüe's elaborate set-up was all ready to go underneath black covering—and the stage manager would guide me through my duties. I'd be out there with the house lights up before the Crüe actually started their set.

Dutifully following the instructions I was given in the production office, I was standing on the floor of the arena, stage left at the bottom of the ramp leading to the top of the stage, when Faster Pussycat's portion of the night ended. As the house lights came up, I was carefully rehearsing my on-stage spiel over and over again in my head while trying not to get run over by the enormous Anvil road cases that thundered down the ramp in clouds of roadie perspiration and grunts. Taking a long look out in the crowd, I saw a sea of the kind of rock humanity that one was apt to witness in these last days of hair metal greatness, before Nirvana came and washed away the spandex-clad sins from the land.

A voice called out my name from the crowd above me in the arena: "Brutus! Hey, Lou Brutus! Whoooh!"

I looked up a few rows to see a black-T-shirted guy with long hair on his head and a white, porcelain bong shaped like a crescent moon in his hand, wildly flailing his arms at me as bong water sloshed onto the two buxom women on either side of him, their hair teased so high to the sky I was mildly shocked they both weren't required to be topped with flashing red safety lights to warn off planes landing at nearby T. F. Green Airport.

"Brutus, dude! I love you! You're the best! Get me backstage to party with you and the band! It'll be Mötley Loü! Whooooh! Let's do it! You are the fucking man! Whoooh!"

Unable to fulfill his request even if I wanted to, I merely shrugged my shoulders and called out, "Sorry, can't do it 'cause the band is going on soon!"

His once glowing opinion of me changed rather quickly.

"Brutus, dude! I hate you! I always hated you. You fucking suck, you fucking pussy! Eat shit and die, motherfucker! You eat ass on the air! Fucking poser! Fuck yoooou!"

My public, how they love me.

I then felt a heavy hand on my shoulder and someone spoke into my ear, "It's show time."

I followed the stage manager up the ramp, and we stopped on the side of the stage. I quickly surveyed the scene.

94

It was a massive, tiered set design with the drums on their skyscraper-like riser. There were vocal microphones out front and a wall of amps in the back so high that all of East Berlin could easily have been kept at bay behind them. The hall was filling up with metal heads in the harsh white houselights of the intermission. The nearby roadies eyed me with an unhidden mixture of scorn and boredom.

The stage manager spun me around to face him nose to nose. He put a hand on each of my shoulders. He spoke quickly, but forcefully and clearly, as he no doubt believed that those at the bottom rung of the entertainment ladder were the biggest morons on the planet.

"You are going to walk directly out to the center microphone. You will not adjust the microphone stand. You will not touch anything. You will not take any guitar picks. You will not grab any drumsticks. You will not say a word until you are told to do so. You will hear the sound man give you the go-ahead. You will hear his voice come up from under your feet because the monitors are mounted inside the floor. You will speak for no more than thirty seconds. You will then walk directly back to me here. You will follow my instructions, or I'll personally beat the living shit out of you."

I was absolutely sure he would and could do it.

My knees buckled beneath me as my final attempt to run through the on-stage banter in my head was interrupted by a quick shove from the stage manager and a roughly blurted "go!"

Stumbling toward the center microphone, I began to worry. Did my time walking out there count toward my thirty seconds? Did the walk back? Would I hear the sound man's voice clearly or would I miss my cue and end up standing center stage mutely until the stage manager came to publicly stomp me into a fruity, juicy pulp while all of Rhode Island's head-bangers hooted their approval?

Panic. I had nearly reached the microphone. Panic. I looked out at the crowd. Panic. I heard a voice beneath my feet.

"Okay, radio boy. Start talkin."

I stepped up to the microphone, but before I could utter a sound, the voice spoke again beneath my feet.

"Don't forget to mention Nick the Pig."

My body and brain stopped cold.

Who or what was Nick the Pig? Was there a band before Faster Pussycat that I hadn't known about? Was he a roadie? Was it the band's mascot?

As these questions flashed across my mind and icy beads of flop sweat formed on my forehead, I had a clear vision of the stage manager pummeling my face with a metal guitar slide and my teeth scattering about the stage to be thrown out later to the crowd by the band as souvenirs.

I unfroze and began blathering.

"Ladies and gentlemen, brothers and sisters, friends of the revolution! Welcome to the capital of western civilization: the Providence Civic Center! I'm Lou Brutus from WHJY!"

At the mention of my name, a deep-throated roar rose up from nearly half a dozen people in the crowd. Emboldened, I pressed on.

"Give it up to Faster Pussycat for opening the show! Mötley Crüe is going to hit the stage in a few minutes! Thanks for coming out tonight!"

Yeah, I know. Pretty bland, but I'd like to see you do better after having not one but two members of the crew threaten to beat the living shit out of you in the last few minutes.

Thinking myself finished, I stepped back from the microphone, but then remembered the words of the soundman and leaned forward once more.

"God bless Nick the Pig!"

With those last words echoing out over the ten thousand plus in the arena, my task was done, and I scurried back to the side of the stage.

The stage manager and the now smiling roadies, some flashing double thumbs up, enthusiastically greeted me there.

He grinned. "How the hell do you know about Nick the Pig?"

At first, I mistook his grin as maniacal and feared he was about to beat the living shit out of me. "Honestly, I have no idea what it means. The sound man told me to mention Nick the Pig, so I did. Please don't hurt me," I wheedled.

He put his arm around me and led me back toward the ramp.

"Hurt you? You're a hero now."

It was then that I noticed many of the roadies were wearing black T-shirts with a cartoon drawing of a gigantic pink pig on them, the name "Nick the Pig" emblazoned along the top. Many of the roadies paused for a moment from their last minute, preshow duties to give me curiously evil smiles or yell "Nick the Fucking Pig!"

We reached the bottom of the ramp and the stage manager stopped and asked, "Do you wanna see Nick the Pig?"

"Hell, yeah," I said.

I had just made a terrible, terrible mistake.

We now walked underneath the stage and into a maze of narrow, dark hallways and miniature rooms, each one a nerve center for a different facet of the show. This was where crewmembers would be monitoring or controlling every aspect of the enormous production, right underneath where the band would soon be playing.

We entered one of the rooms, and my eyes were blinded for a moment by the bright banks of video monitors that lined the inside. Being the towering intellect that I am, I quickly deduced this was where the video portion of the show was run from. You can't get anything by me.

The crew looked up at the stage manager, who smiled and said, "Show our friend here Nick the Pig."

A dark chuckling rose up from the men at the board, filled with banks of colored lights and levers. One of them pressed a button and pointed toward a monitor.

And that was when I saw him.

Nick the Pig.

Nick wasn't a man. No, Nick was not human at all. He would not be confused with the character of the same name from *Scarface*. Nick was actually a pig with four hooves and a curly tail. However, he wasn't a regular-sized swine. He was enormous. I would swear by the same God who cursed me with his porky visage that Nick must have weighed nearly half a ton. Nick was not the cute, cuddly kind of pig who might be seen on an Easter card or saving Farmer Hoggett's farm in a *Babe* film. He was a hairy pig. A beastly pig. An ugly pig.

One other thing, Nick the Pig was a porn star.

I'm not talking the kind of animal on animal sex you used to see on the old Saturday Night Live sketch "E. Buzz Miller's Animal Kingdom" with Dan Akroyd starring as a sleazebag hosting nature films of various beasts copulating in the wild. Nick the Pig was on the video screen before me banging away at a bevy of women.

Human women.

I threw up a little in my mouth. The video crew devilishly laughed. I had a vision of what hell was going to look like if I ever went there. It was a vision filled with fire, brimstone, and uncircumcised hog dick.

Don't get me wrong. I feel I'm fairly liberal in my sexual mores. "Live and let live" is my motto. I am of the opinion that people should be allowed to live their lives the way they want. However, I also believe that a woman's glory hole is no place for a pig's weenie.

I'm old-fashioned that way.

I never did find out the actual title of the film. I imagine it had a moniker like "Pigs in Blankets," "Behind the Green Barn Door," or "Once Upon A Time in Porkywood." I don't remember how much I watched, but it wasn't a lot.

My brain shut down after a few moments. The next thing I knew, I was curled up in a ball, sitting on the hallway floor backstage, where I rocked back and forth muttering to myself. My right eye twitched uncontrollably.

The band had started their set with "Kickstart My Heart" and the onstage bombs shook the arena, but it was several songs into the set before I could rally myself to walk out on unsteady legs and watch the show.

Say what you will about Mötley Crüe, but those boys gave you your money's worth. It was a phenomenal production. While they may not musically be everyone's cup of tea, you can at least see where they reinvested your ticket money for your enjoyment. You have to respect a band like that.

Even if their road crew did enjoy watching women gorge on uncooked pork chop.

During the set, around the time the twitching in my right eye had stopped, the radio station's program director,

Bill Weston, tracked me down to let me know that the band's lead singer, Vince Neil, would be joining me in the studio the following afternoon before the second sold-out show.

One thing I always try to do for an interview subject is attempt to think of something to warm them up before we go on air. It can be an inside joke, a bit of knowledge regarding a little-known hobby, or anything else that will let them know I am knowledgeable regarding their life so that they hopefully feel comfortable while speaking to me.

My mind raced as I tried to think up what I could do to break the ice the next day with Vince Neil. As the band hammered away onstage at hits like "Shout at the Devil," "Looks That Kill," and "Girls, Girls, Girls," a plan began to form in my mind.

I would record a song about Nick the Pig.

It didn't have to be an original song. I would be better off doing a short, parody version of a Mötley Crüe tune. I could arrive early the next day to the radio studio, bang out the song, and play it for Vince before we went on the air. The idea wasn't to make something that was "Weird Al" Yankovic quality in its production values, just something down and dirty to give Vince a laugh so he'd open up on the air.

However, the question remained: "What song would I use?"

The band had just finished their first encore song of "Home Sweet Home" and gone into the title track of their current album when the answer came to me in a blur of music and words that rhymed with pork.

The album title *Dr. Feelgood* would become *Dr. Nick the Pig.*

I've written hundreds of parody songs. Some of them have been quite good and ended up going viral. Some have been featured on network news programs like my Clinton/

Lewinsky songs "A-Monica the Beautiful" and "The Star-Spangled Boner," which ended up on ABC News. While parody is considered the lowest form of comedy, I'm quite proud of some of my work in this field.

However, "Dr. Nick the Pig" was a piece of shit.

It featured lyrics like, *"He's the one they call Dr. Nick the Pig. He's the one that makes ya go, 'Sooie!'"* I don't remember much else other than the rest was probably even stupider. Well, if that's possible. It may rank as the most god-awful parody song ever produced. The vocal cancellation method I used to remove the singing from the original didn't do a very clean job, but since I didn't intend it to be heard by anyone except a single play for Vince Neil, I wasn't concerned.

I arrived early the following day to the studio and began work on the song and finished just in time for the start of my shift. Vince got there in the late afternoon looking like he had just rolled out of bed but was pleasant if a bit crispy. There was a long song already playing on the station that we'd have to wait out before he and I could go on-air, so I had time to warm him up and play the song.

It was as he was autographing the green *Dr. Feelgood* medical smock I purchased the night before at the concession stand when I asked if I could play him something special off the air. Though probably fearing I'd force him to listen to a band I was in myself that I'd then beg him to sign to a record contract, he still kindly agreed.

When the opening notes of "Dr. Feelgood" began he gave me a bit of a "what the fuck" look. Then he heard the opening line, *"Curl-tailed Nicky is a well-hung swine, He squeals at Hollywood and Vine,"* and his eyes widened. When the chorus began with its three-part harmonies on the word *"Sooie,"* he leaned in toward me with an incredulous face and asked, "How the fuck do you know about Nick the Pig?!?!"

When I quickly relayed my pork-soaked tale from the previous evening, he cackled with evil glee and said, "You gotta play this on the radio to start the interview! Oh, and I'll need five copies to bring back to the arena with me."

The time with Vince on the station was a smashing success after this greatest of all icebreakers. I was happy in hindsight that I hadn't included any four-letter words in the lyrics that would have had to have been edited out on the fly. Vince left with a handful of white cassette tapes (this was the eighties) with the radio station logo neatly printed on the sides and the words "Dr. Nick the Pig" scrawled over it in blood red Magic Marker. Vince promised to get me my very own Nick the Pig shirt. Sadly, I never did receive it. The last time I was with Vince in early 2019 to talk about the Mötley Crüe biopic *The Dirt*, I asked him about the shirt. He just smiled at me blankly with no recollection of any of this. I wasn't surprised, but I was disappointed. I had always held out a bit of hope that I'd one day get the shirt and comb eBay to this day trying to find one.

Later that evening, I walked into the Providence Civic Center and I heard something. It was a strangely familiar song. "Dr. Nick the Pig" was playing on the PA system for the crowd to hear! My all-access pass jumped now to the beat of my heart proudly pounding beneath. As I walked up to the side of the stage to get ready for my second night of emceeing, the road crew pointed at me and cried out, "It's him! It's the Nick the Pig guy!" They slapped me on the back and high-fived me. I had been accepted as one of their own.

My blood rushed. My spirit soared. My animal porn song was a smash.

I hit the stage with far bolder patter than the night before.

"Hey, motherfuckers!!! I'm Lou Brutus from WHJY and Mötley Fucking Crüe is gonna be out here soon to pound your asses into submission!!! Until then, God Bless Nick the Fucking Pig!!!"

I drop a lot of f-bombs when I get excited.

The audience cheered. The roadies cheered. The stage manager cheered. I then high-stepped off stage and down the ramp where I stopped and basked in my own glory. I had scored points with a major band and their crew. I had gone on stage before thousands like a champion. I had created the greatest pig sex song of all time.

I closed my eyes and turned my face to the heavens. I lifted both arms and threw my fists up into the air. I thought to myself, "Oh, mighty Rock Gods! Give me a sign that you will smile on me forever!"

At that moment, I felt a splash on my face. As I stumbled forward, eyes squeezed shut ensuring no equilibrium, I wretched a bit on the warm liquid that had poured into my nose. I threw out one arm to keep from landing on my face and hit the floor. Then I recognized the horrible, stale, dank smell of the liquid. It was bong water.

I opened my eyes to a slightly blurry vision and looked upward. Above me, through the haze, I saw a familiar face from the previous evening. It was the long-haired guy in the black T-shirt, and he was now holding an upturned white porcelain bong shaped like a crescent moon with the last drops of water dripping out. He called out to me above the din just as the lights went down.

"HEY, LOOOOOUUUU!!! YOU SUUUUUUUUUUCK!!!"

THE TIME KEITH RICHARDS DRAINED THE LIFE ENERGY OUT OF MY BODY THROUGH THE PALM OF MY HAND

voo·doo
n. pl. **voo·doos**
1. A religion practiced chiefly in Caribbean countries, especially Haiti, syncretized from Roman Catholic ritual elements and the animism and magic of slaves from West Africa, in which a supreme God rules a large pantheon of local and tutelary deities, deified ancestors, and saints, who communicate with believers in dreams, trances, and ritual possessions. Also called *vodoun*.
2. A charm, fetish, spell, or curse holding magic power for adherents of voodoo.
3. A practitioner, priest, or priestess of voodoo.

I SWEAR TO YOU the following story is true. Every accursed word of it.

On September 22, 1994, the Rolling Stones brought their Voodoo Lounge Tour to Veterans Stadium in Philadelphia. It was an evening that began with me mocking the Spinal Tap–like silliness of the "Voodoo" moniker but ended with a fight for my life against the black magic it referred to.

At the time, I was doing the late shift at legendary rock station WMMR. It was through that connection I had scored an elusive backstage pass to the Stones's meet and greet that night. No guest, just me. He travels fastest who travels alone, and a rolling stone gathers no moss, so who was I to argue?

As I walked through the labyrinth of featureless cement tunnels beneath the stadium, I slipped my teal and silver hologram backstage pass into a large, see-through plastic envelope that hung on a lanyard around my neck. It's a habit I had picked up to take better care of the "sticker" passes that were usually given out to single-night guests on a tour. Security insisted they be worn, but that meant peeling off the back, which meant a higher chance of damage and difficulty storing it later, so I began using this alternate method. I took better care of my passes then I did my immortal soul, and on this fateful Thursday night it almost cost me.

The Rolling Stones backstage meetings are not intimate affairs. They are usually corporate sponsored in large rooms, with no autographs and no one-on-one pictures. Large groups of people are brought in waves lasting about five minutes. A lucky few get a couple seconds of chit-chat with a band member, then there's a big group photo, and finally you're rushed out to make room for the next group.

It's not optimum, but it's the Rolling Stones. My editor suggested that I should add, "You can't always get what you want, but sometimes you get what you need." I beat him with a truncheon for his dad-joke insolence.

My group was to be the last to meet the band. I saw a few friendly faces standing around in the hallway, including fellow Philly DJs Matt Cord, Ray Koob, and Ed Sciaky. We made small talk and exchanged Stones stories as we waited for the group in front of us to finish. Whenever I brought up the tour name, I put a sarcastic emphasis on the word "voodoo." Rolling Stones or not, I thought it kind of a goofy name.

The group before us began to file out from behind the line of temporary, flimsy blue curtains that separated us from the band area. Most everyone had giddy looks on their faces. I heard the usual comments as they walked by, "I'm never washing this hand again," "they're a lot shorter in person," and "Charlie Watts looks like a goddamned wax statue," being some of the more common.

Bringing up the rear of the exiting group was a guy on his knees being dragged out in between two security guards. I remember that he was wearing an old Rolling Stones concert T-shirt from their 1981 American Tour, which played it's opening gig at Philly's JFK Stadium. I was there that day.

The guy looked drugged out and pathetic as he was pulled along the ground. As he went by, he looked up with half-lidded, pitiful eyes and tried to mouth something to me. I thought he was saying "roooock." How typical. However, before I could be sure, I noticed the rest of my group were in the room already, so I turned heel and followed them. It was only later in the night, as I tried to piece together the living nightmare I had encountered, that I realized he was saying "ruuuuun."

I walked in and there they were, up close and personal, the Rolling Stones.

Jagger had the biggest group of admirers around him. I'd seen him up close once before across the street at JFK Stadium at Live Aid. More on that later in the book. Like many other huge celebs I'd encountered, he used humor to put nervous people at ease. He made everyone chuckle a bit, brought the tension down, and then could have a few human moments with them. Some of those standing in the semicircle looked like they were ready to drop to their knees and blow him on the spot. Lucky bastard. What a life.

Drummer Charlie Watts had a small group of music nerd lookin' guys around him. No girls, just nerds. In the scant moments they had been together, Charlie and his acolytes were already deep into a conversation about snare drum heads. Fuckin' drum geeks. They never grow out of it.

Ronnie Wood was the most animated of the lot. He had a number of folks with him smiling and nodding their heads. The last I had seen him in such close proximity, the two of us were doing shots of Jack Daniels out of paper cups at the back of the manager's office in Borders Books on Chestnut Street here in Philadelphia. A damned fine fellow that Ronnie Wood. Great graphic artist, too.

I was going over to see if I could get a word in with Ronnie when I saw...him. Standing in the corner. Alone. Not a soul around him. An ash the length of an entire cigarette dangling from the corner of his lip, waiting for his permission to fall to the ground.

Keith Richards.

If there was ever a back-alley knife fight between Steve McQueen, Captain Kidd, and Chuck Berry with Dr. Frankenstein taking the sliced-off body parts to sew together into a complete human being, that human being would be Keith Richards.

The living embodiment of cool.

No one else in the room had seemed to notice him. It was as if the rest of them didn't even see the guy. I couldn't believe my luck. I was going to be able to speak to Keith Richards for the first time in my life.

My mind raced for a subject to open the conversation with. That's a very important thing when making small talk with rock stars. You don't need to tell them what a huge fan you are. They can already safely (and modestly) assume you're a fan as you probably wouldn't be at their show if you weren't. If you blubber at them, you look like a douche. Just be cool and pleasant.

I quickly settled on asking Keith if he had heard from Waddy Wachtel recently. Waddy is a hot shit guitarist whose playing I first came to admire in the band of my old friend Warren Zevon. I had last seen Waddy play live as part of Keith's solo group The X-Pensive Winos at The Orpheum in Boston the year before. It was the perfect conversation starter. It showed I was a fan, that I knew the players, and that I was cool. Well, I thought so anyway. "Keef" and I would be chatting like old mates in no time.

I walked across the room to Keith and held out my hand.

"Hi, Keith. My name is Lou and it's a pleasure to—" but I never finished my sentence.

Several things began to happen the moment Keith and I locked hands. The first is that the rest of the room plunged into near darkness. Then the people around us reduced to mere shades while he and I stood in cold, harsh shafts of light.

As I looked up at him, I noticed his eyes. His terrible, terrible eyes. They throbbed with a hellish amber glow. A leering grin spread across his wrinkled face. The wider he grinned, the more the wrinkles opened, until they began to look like valleys. Valleys of the Damned. It seemed I heard voices rising up from the valleys. Were they human or demon, I know not. I only can say that they will haunt me for the rest of my life and that if an unmerciful God wills me to the fiery depths when I die, the cries of whatever creatures have been consigned there for eternity will be familiar to my ears.

The shafts of light we stood in began to pulsate.

Keith continued to stare at me with his amber eyes and wicked grin until I could take the horror no more. I tried in vain to pull my hand away, but we were locked together in preternatural bond, held tight by dark magnetism. I looked down at my hand and saw that, as incredible as it sounds, it was aging. My hand was adding years right before my eyes. It was shriveling. I looked up at Keith and I saw the valleys were now closing, the lines were fading, his face gaining youth by the moment as my life's energy was sucked out through the palm of my hand to replenish his body.

His shaft of light now grew brighter, while mine began to flicker and weaken. I fell to my knees.

I can be certain there was no Dorian Gray picture of Keith Richards tucked away in the attic of some English estate or French chateau he owned. The fiend was draining the very spark of mortality from his fans each night in order to elongate his life of rock and roll debauchery. Sucking sustenance for energy with a flick of his wrist was probably a regular ritual to give him the strength for each performance. I knew then what a can of Red Bull felt like.

Finally, with the last shred of strength I had left, I wrenched my hand away from his. My clothes were soaked with sweat. My chest was heaving. Pain wracked my body. Blisters rose from the palm of my hand.

Keith leaned over and whispered in my ear, the only words I've ever heard him speak in person before or since. His mocking, crackling, cackling voice like the sound of stone slabs grinding together in a dark, dank mausoleum.

"What a drag it is getting old—eh, mate?"

Then, still grinning, he winked at me and snapped his head quickly to one side, causing his neck to crack with the sound of a splintering two-by-four and sending his cigarette ash flying down into my eye.

Then he was gone. I don't mean he walked away. He just... vanished.

By the time I had the strength to look up again the two security guards I had seen earlier flanked me. It had only been a few moments since I saw them previously, but it seemed like a lifetime. The first looked at the second and said, "Shit. Another one. Can't any of these assholes hold their booze?"

I didn't protest as they dragged me out to the sidewalk into the cool September evening air. By the time the band launched into their opening number of "Not Fade Away" I was in a cab on my way to the colonial era Christ Church near the corner of Second and Market. I shouldered my way through the ancient wooden doors, stumbled to the altar, fell to my knees, and I prayed.

When I finished, I lifted up my hand to examine the blisters. What I saw gave me a shock for the pustules had formed a word. A single word that I would carry on the palm of my hand for months to come and in my brain through countless nightmares across the years.

The word?

"Voodoo."

THE TIME OUR TOUR BUS RAN OVER A GUY ON THE NEW JERSEY TURNPIKE

IN EARLY APRIL OF 2011 I got a call from Corey Taylor, the aforementioned lead singer for both Slipknot and Stone Sour, with a kind invitation to join the latter band on the road as they supported their then latest album *Audio Secrecy*. While the trip was fun, it led to one of the most bizarre events ever in my travels.

As I always enjoyed my time on tour with Slipknot or Stone Sour, I readily agreed to hit the road again. The moniker for this particular jaunt was "The Avalanche Tour." The full lineup consisted of Stone Sour, Theory of A Deadman, Halestorm, Skillet, and Art of Dying. As I knew all these groups very well from interviewing them since they were baby bands, I was confident I would see many friendly faces.

The Stone Sour lineup at this time also included guitarist Jim Root. Like Corey, Jim was a member of Slipknot and one of the people I've spent the most time with on my travels. A tall and imposing person physically but soft-spoken and thoughtful in tone, Jim is another of my favorite people in the music world. The other guitarist in the band was (and is) Josh Rand. Along with being a quiet and intense person, Josh is a key member of Stone Sour, as he works diligently on music while Slipknot is in active mode. Roy Mayorga the amazing drummer and multi-instrumentalist was beating the skins while bass duties were being handled by Jason Christopher, filling in for the recently departed Shawn Economaki.

After consulting a band itinerary against my work schedule, Corey and I figured it would be easiest for me to hop aboard the tour at the New York City show at the Hammerstein Ballroom on Friday, April 29. I could travel overnight to an outdoor concert in Bangor, Maine, then head back down the coast for a Sunday night gig at the Mohegan Sun Arena in Connecticut. The next performance after that was in Richmond, Virginia, so the bus could drop me at my office at SiriusXM Radio in Washington, DC, early Monday morning. As my workplace had a gym with a locker room and shower, I could wash the tour grime off my body and not stink up my office.

Speaking of which, not showering can become a very big issue during a bus or van tour. You can sometimes go days between hotel rooms, and dressing rooms often do not have a shower. It's the main reason I often equate band touring to camping. It's a helluva lotta fun for a few days, but after a few gigs without anyone bathing, you can start to identify the band members in the dark by their smell. Blech. All you want to do is go home to wash the funk off before you knock somebody out with armpit stench. How the fuck people do this for a living is beyond me. Sometimes I want to grab a band member, douse them in disinfectant, and shake them by the shoulders, screaming, "YOU PEOPLE LIVE LIKE

ANIMALS!" Being slapped in the face by rock star stank can be a great reminder that you should have gone into a more normal line of work. More about this than you'd rather know in a later chapter.

Another thing to know if you're going to travel with a rock band on tour is that it's very important to stay the proper amount of time. If your trip is too short, you don't feel like you've had a rich enough experience. If you're out too long, you might start to get the feeling you've overstayed your welcome.

However, this trip seemed like it would be just the right length, so I had a big grin on my face as I showed up in the tour manager's office at the theatre in New York City to grab my pass. The show was sold out, the buzz from the crowd filled the air, and the backstage was brimming with friends and family. That's one of the things about shows in New York; there are a fuck ton of guests. The record companies are there, so the entire staff will usually show up. There is a slew of music media, so they all show up, and family members who live elsewhere often love to travel in, as it's always a big gig. Plus, it's New York City, so there is plenty of fun to be had. It was a great night to be a part of rock 'n' roll.

I said quick hellos to everyone as I dashed from the office with my pass, dumped my bag on the bus, and ran with my camera out to the photo pit. By now I had begun taking an entry-level digital camera on the road with me. I can't even imagine the great kindness rock stars were taking on me back then in this respect, as I had very little skill at shooting music events. And lemme tell ya something, if you think mosh pits in New York City can be crazy as fuck, they ain't got doodly-squat on the photo pit. With so many magazines, fanzines, websites, blogs, and newspapers in town, virtually every photo pit is jammed with photogs in NYC.

The entire slate of bands killed it that night. There were throngs of fans still surrounding the buses as we pulled away into the late-night Manhattan streets at 2:00 a.m. Our bus was driven by a friendly Canadian fellow named Wade.

I had been going for close to twenty hours straight on nothing but black coffee and adrenaline, so while everyone else discussed the night's gig in the front lounge, I stumbled back to the midpoint of the bus where my bunk would be for three nights. I changed into some black sweat clothes, my preferred clothing to wear for days straight on tour, climbed into my bunk, and passed out.

There is an art to sleeping on a moving tour bus. First of all, you want your feet to face in the direction that the bus is moving. That way if the bus stops short it's your feet taking the brunt of gravity and not the top of your noggin. You also need to get used to the movement of the bus. Once the driver has you on an interstate it's not too bad. There is a gentle swaying motion that can rock you to sleep. It can take a bit of getting used to the first night, but after that it actually helps you fall asleep, like the sound of the ocean in a seaside cottage.

The first day, for the most part, passed like any normal tour stop. The outdoor gig in Bangor, Maine, at Waterfront Park was great fun though a little chilly for the bands. Temps were only in the fifties, but the sky was blue and after a winter in Central Maine, these conditions must have seemed like Spring Break in Cancun to the Bangorians. They frolicked about in shorts and T-shirts while I stuck my hands down my jeans to keep my balls from shrinking in the cold to the size of raisins. I snapped a lot of pictures and hung with the bands. I proudly felt like a tour veteran.

However, there was one unfortunate event in Maine that foreshadowed the nastiness on my final night with the tour. I was in the catering tent when a bloodcurdling scream rose up from nearby. The first thing I thought was that it sounded like something from a Stephen King novel. I had had him on my mind as he lived in Bangor, was a well-known metal fan, and I hoped maybe he would show up that day. The grim reality was far less fun. Apparently, a local man working as a roadie got run over by a forklift and it snapped his leg. As I came back down from catering they were wheeling him on a stretcher toward the ambulance.

Other than that, the next couple of days passed smoothly with a lot of laughs, even though Stephen King didn't show up. We arrived at Mohegan Sun Arena in Uncasville, Connecticut, early Sunday and happily invaded the beautiful dressing rooms and the showers therein. The show kicked ass and I said my goodbyes to everyone on the tour that night, knowing that the Stone Sour bus would be dropping me in DC sometime early the next morning while everyone slept. I climbed into my bunk while the bus still sat in the underground loading dock area beneath the casino. I'd sleep till the bus was near my office in DC and then hop off the tour quietly.

But it didn't quite work out that way.

When I awoke the bus was stopped but the engine was still running. Though it didn't feel like I had slept that long, I assumed that we were in Washington and that I'd reached my destination. I heard someone moving outside my bunk, so I slid back my curtain and found myself face to face with Jim Root.

I sleepily slurred to him, "Hey, Jim. Are we in DC? I gotta grab my bag and get off the bus."

Jim replied, "No, we're not in DC. We're actually stopped in the middle of the New Jersey Turnpike, where our bus just ran over a suicidal crackhead."

What. The. Fuck.

I thought he was kidding. I thought perhaps I had misheard him. No, I know what I heard. He must be kidding.

"Dude, that's a fucked-up thing to say. Cut that shit out. Grab my bag so I can get off the bus."

"No, Lou. We are stopped in the middle of the highway blocking all the lanes. There's a New Jersey State Trooper in the front lounge. Come on up and say hello. He's really nice!"

At this point I jumped out of my bunk and headed for the front lounge. When I walked in, there he was. A New Jersey State Trooper who easily stood eleven feet tall and six feet wide. Okay, maybe not that big, but this guy was huge. The top of his trooper hat nearly scraped the lounge ceiling as he smiled politely and held out his hand.

"Good morning, sir. Are you okay?"

Before I could answer I looked out the side window of the lounge. The bus was on a slight diagonal with some other stopped vehicles blocking the entire southbound New Jersey Turnpike. If you're familiar with the roadway (being from New Jersey I know every inch of it), we were a few miles north of exit four near Cherry Hill. I was looking out the right side of the bus north into three lanes of traffic backed up as far as the eye could see.

What. The. Fuck.

"I'm fine, Trooper. Thanks for asking."

Here's a quick aside about dealing with state troopers around the country: These men and women are not a part of the "regular" police force where they live and work. They are elite law enforcement. They receive more intense training and are generally held to a much higher standard than the local hometown cop who pulls you over for doing twenty-six MPH in a twenty-five-MPH zone. If you call any of them "officer" instead of "trooper" they might react much in the same way you would if someone had spit in your coffee. If you want a surefire way of getting a state trooper to write you a ticket when they pull you over, call them "officer." I dare you.

The trooper smiled at my use of terminology and continued. "We want to make sure everyone on your bus is okay. Your driver did an outstanding job keeping you all alive and avoiding what could have been a more tragic situation."

Wade, our driver, was standing next to him. Thinking he might need consoling over what had happened I put my hand on his shoulder and asked, "Are you all right?"

Wade looked up and answered in his thick Canadian accent, "Yah, I'm fine. Fuck that asshole. He could have gotten us all killed!"

To be honest, at this point I was assuming someone had died, so the vibe of the conversation seemed a bit, ummm, *unrestrained* to me. Then the trooper laid out the whole story for us as everyone else had started to gather in the lounge rubbing sleep from their eyes. We began to understand his relatively happy mood considering the southbound traffic was probably backed up all the way to where we had played in Maine two days ago.

Dawn had been starting to break over the highway and the three lanes of traffic were moving smoothly. Wade had the CB radio on at a low volume to keep an ear on road conditions. Suddenly, he saw brake lights flashing ahead and heard bits of static-y conversation from the speaker.

"GUY IN ROAD...TRYING...WANTS...GET HIT... SCREAMING...JESUS!!!"

Wade began to slow the bus down. As you can imagine, tour buses can't stop on a dime. He noticed traffic ahead was swerving out of the center of the highway so he inched our bus as far over to the left as he could and applied more brake. This section of the Turnpike had only a foot or two of extra pavement on the side before the Jersey barrier that separated our southbound side from the northbound traffic. There was nowhere else to go. Wade used every millimeter he could without hitting the center divide.

Then Wade saw him! A man walking up the center of the New Jersey Turnpike, looking up to the sky and yelling something as he stretched out his arms in a Christ-like pose.

The man was getting closer.

The bus was slowing down.

Wade stomped the brake.

It was going to be close.

Bus almost stopped.

Razor thin margin.

THUD!

We hit the guy.

But we had only caught him on the arm with our side mirror and knocked him to the ground. The bus finally came to a complete stop askew the highway.

Wade leapt from his seat, opened the door, and jumped out onto the pavement.

A wild-eye man with disheveled clothes lay on the ground screaming.

"I WANNA MEET JESUS. I WANNA MEET JESUS!"

The troopers arrived within moments. When they approached the man on the ground, he rolled underneath the bus to get away from them. An ambulance eventually fought its way through the traffic. They got the man out from underneath the bus, onto a stretcher, and took him off to a hospital.

We got our bus off to the right side of the turnpike and traffic began to move, albeit slowly. Our state trooper got back on the bus and then explained to us a term known as "suicide by traffic."

Turns out there had recently been a rash of suicides on the NJT, people running out into traffic to purposely get run over. The trooper explained he had one of these cases just a couple of weeks before where a drug addict had murdered his girlfriend and then committed suicide by running in front of an eighteen-wheeler. The truck driver had been unable to stop but did make eye contact with the man just before running him over. The drug addict was dead. The driver was going to need counseling and might not ever be able to work his profession. A tragedy inside of a tragedy.

The trooper assumed this was another case of someone on drugs trying to do themselves in. The man had been walking through the lanes of traffic yelling, "I wanna meet Jesus!" The trooper had given Jim Root all of this background before I came out, and this led to the "suicidal crackhead" assumption. In actuality, I later learned that the man was a truck driver who had been heading northbound on the Turnpike that morning. It was assumed he had been up without sleep for a few days driving and jackknifed his truck. Instead of staying with it, he went a little crazy, abandoned it, and began walking up the highway.

I was never able to learn the man's fate. I did receive word from some friends in New Jersey law enforcement that he was treated for minor injuries in the hospital before being taken for psychiatric evaluation. After that, the trail went cold. I hope he got help and got his life together, though I'm pretty sure Wade wanted to kick him in the nut sack.

We were soon back on our way toward DC and Richmond. There were, of course, no charges for Wade. Frankly, I think they should have given him a fucking medal. This incident turned out as well as it did because of his steel nerves behind the wheel. This could have been a horrible event for any one of a large number of people that morning but was not because of the big, Canadian balls of our driver.

One last note, this was the *second* time I had escaped death on the very same stretch of the New Jersey Turnpike. In 1982 when I was an intern for WMMR in Philadelphia, I was returning from a performance by The Who, The Clash, and The David Johansen Group at Shea Stadium in New York. That day I had driven from Central Jersey down to Philly to pick up my coworker Paulette Babikan, and then drove up to Queens, New York, for the show before returning back south. This was a bad idea. I fell asleep behind the wheel of my 1973 Volkswagen Beetle and woke up doing 360s in the middle of the turnpike.

Back in those days, there was still a section of grass along either side of the guardrail between the north and southbound sides. My car went forward into the grass, which piled up and formed a barrier between my car and the metal beam divider. We came to an abrupt stop and the engine stalled. There wasn't a scratch on the car, just some dirt and grass along the front bumper.

I am dead serious when I tell you that a voice then spoke very clearly in my head, "You thank God that you're alive."

"Thank you, God," I said out loud. Then I started the car and drove safely away.

I don't know who watches over me, but I'm very thankful that they do.

THE TIME STEVIE NICKS LOCKED HERSELF IN THE BATHROOM WITH MY GIRLFRIEND, WHICH LED ME TO FEAR I'D GET WHACKED BY THE MOB

THERE WERE SEVERAL YEARS as a young man where I had a long succession of girlfriends enamored with Stevie Nicks of Fleetwood Mac. Collectively, I refer to them as Little Stevie and the Disciples of Nicks. They would dress like Stevie, with the black top hat and long, flowing clothing. They would do their hair like Stevie. They would wear their makeup like Stevie. It was obsessive. Now, I didn't consciously plan my life for this. I didn't fall in love with women who worshipped her on purpose, my love life just worked out that way. Little did I know that bringing one of these women to meet Stevie would put me in fear for my life.

This particular incident occurred in May of 1986 at the Spectrum in Philadelphia while Nicks was on the first leg of her "Rock A Little" solo tour. The opening act for the night was an Austrian band called Opus. The city loved her, and she would be back at the same venue a couple of months later with the great Peter Frampton as support. I'm pretty sure I went to that show as well, though I don't have a ticket stub from it.

I had first seen Stevie onstage when she performed with Fleetwood Mac across the street from the Spectrum at JFK Stadium during the "Rumors" tour in 1978. I was still in school at the time and the group was riding as high as a band could. The show was sold out with over a hundred thousand attending, including school chums Bruce Klein, Chuck Grill, and myself. As Bruce's parents were away, we—ahem—"borrowed" their *Brady Bunch*–looking wood-paneled station wagon the night before the show. We then took the one-hour southbound trip down the New Jersey Turnpike, over the Walt Whitman Bridge, and into the stadium parking lot. There were about a thousand other fans already there and the night was passed in a haze of warm beer and clouds of low-quality-weed smoke. The concert also featured the Steve Miller Band, former Fleetwood Mac member Bob Welch, and the Sanford-Townsend band whose short set was capped with the tune that entered them into the pantheon of one-hit wonders, "Smoke from a Distant Fire." It was a hot, humid day and a fun show with many in the crowd bringing in full kegs of beer. No joke. Concert security at outdoor festivals back then just didn't give a hoot in hell. Bruce, Chuck, and I were on the floor of the stadium, slithering through the general admission crowd to get a prime spot in front of Stevie just before the Fleetwood Mac set began. I swear she sang "Landslide" directly to Chuck. Years later when we hit the fortieth anniversary of the show, I found an old picture of the concert and you can see both Chuck and I in the crowd. Sadly, a stage monitor in the shot blocks Bruce's face. I still have my ticket stub from the gig.

So it was great to be able to see Stevie again eight years later on a solo run. I was working at WMMR at the time, and the moment the concert had been announced, I began working to wrangle a couple of backstage passes for after the show. It wasn't easy. Word was she was not doing many meet and greets, but it was imperative for my romantic well-being to get my Nicks-worshipping girlfriend back for a few moments with her heroine.

Before we go any further, I have to make clear that I am not going to mention my now ex-girlfriend by name. She was pure evil. Seriously, she could make a bird fall dead from the sky with just a glance, like a dark-powered enchantress direct from a Stevie Nicks B-side. I fear that putting her name into print would be like breaking the seal on some forbidden religious scroll, leading to a horrific end for all of mankind. For the purpose of this story we shall refer to her as "She Whom We Name Not" or SWWNN for short. I do this for the good of everyone on the planet to protect them from her wicked soul. And I would like to make it clear that everything bad that eventually happened in our relationship was her fault and I was perfect in every way.

By the way, I'm not bitter. Or delusional.

The exact show date was July 23, which fell on a Wednesday night. This made it kinda tough for me as I was working as the radio station's morning show producer in those days, which meant my Soundesign alarm clock radio would be blaring me to wakefulness the next morning at four. Plus, it was commonplace in that era for meet and greets to be held after the performance, not before, as is modus operandi now. The night would be late, and the morning would be fuzzy.

Stevie's performance was tremendous. The word "captivating" gets thrown around a bit too much for my liking when describing artists, but it is spot on for her. Her set included solo hits like "Talk to Me" and "Edge of Seventeen," as well Fleetwood Mac titles like "Dreams" and "Rhiannon." SWWNN and I watched from the press box of the Spectrum before meeting up with the local representative from her record company, Frankie Sciarra of Atlantic Records.

Let's talk for a moment about Frankie Sciarra. At the time, the guy was already an absolute legend among old school record promoters and radio people of the day. It was the record promoter's job to rep an artist or record company, going from radio station to radio station to convince and coerce them into giving up precious playlist slots for airplay. No cell phones. No email. Just face-to-face persistence to get those records played. The more airplay the song got, the more a record promo person would make. Frankie had been in the game a long time and knew how to get things done.

He also scared the living shit out of me.

You have to understand that I was essentially just a kid, so I was in mortal fear of this man who looked and sounded like he had just walked off the screen of a Martin Scorsese film about the music industry. I'm not saying Frankie would have me wrapped up in chain-link fence and dropped into the nearby Delaware River if I did something stupid backstage with Stevie Nicks, I'm just saying that's what my overactive imagination *thought* could happen. Besides, I was low person in seniority at the radio station and me getting back there was a huge imposition and a very nice gesture by Frankie, as it would have been better for him to have someone of rank at WMMR attend.

As the final notes of Stevie's encore "Has Anyone Ever Written Anything for You" were still wafting through the rafters of the arena, Frankie began assembling the small group of local radio VIPs who would attend the audience with Nicks. Each of the big rock radio stations in Philadelphia had been allowed a single pair of passes. SWWNN and I were there under the umbrella of WMMR while the program directors of competing stations of the time, including WYSP, WIOQ, and WPST made up the rest of the group. There were eight of us led down the staircase at the back of the press box, down past Charles who worked the press box of the Spectrum for so many years he became a beloved minor celebrity to local media, and into the bowels of the Spectrum.

Already being a veteran of many backstage meetings in the building, I was very familiar with the room we were led to. It had two doors, including the first door we entered that connected to the main hallway that ran underneath the entirety of the oblong Spectrum. A second door led to a short hallway and a second room that matched ours and was used that night for Stevie's dressing room. The short hallway also had a shared bathroom off of it for the two rooms.

Sciarra lined us all up then pulled me aside for a brief word.

"I've got all these fucking program directors here and it's VERY IMPORTANT they have time with Stevie. When she walks in, you and your girlfriend are gonna go first," he said in a hushed but insistently fear-inspiring whisper. "Shake her hand, say hello, get an autograph, and then get the fuck out of here." Fearing his wrath, I quickly nodded in agreement. Because I had to get up early, I wanted to beat a hasty retreat myself.

A few moments later the door opened and there she was. Stevie Nicks. As entrancing as she was onstage, she was even more captivating up close. I'd tell you that she walked into the room, but my recollection is that she *glided on air* atop her platform boots. And she was beautiful. Like an elfin warrior princess from a long-ago fairy tale wrapped in flowing scarves with a golden light about her. Stevie seemed to me to be a vision of grace, dignity, and beauty.

Until I noticed the look on her face of complete and utter fucking boredom.

I believe I understood why. Far too often, she was subjected to these meet and greets with local radio programmers. Some of these folks were nice while others could be self-important toads used to having their loathsome behinds kissed in exchange for radio airplay. Some couldn't name one song outside of the current single from an artist whose livelihood depended on their goodwill. So it was completely understandable to me why Stevie's eyes glazed over when she saw us.

Until Stevie noticed She Whom We Name Not.

In a room filled with jaded radio programmers, here was an obvious fan of Stevie's music. SWWNN could have swapped outfits with Nicks and no one would be the wiser. Black hat, long scarves, flowing skirt, platform boots. She was dressed more like Stevie than Stevie was. It was probably a rare opportunity at one of these things for Stevie to have some real human interaction as opposed to the usual music business blitherings.

Brushing past Frankie Sciarra, who was trying to do the initial introductions, Nicks went right to SWWNN and gave her a hug.

"I'm so happy to meet you. My name is Stevie."

"Hi, Stevie! I'm SWWNN!"

"I love your outfit and your makeup," continued Nicks.

"Thank you! I design and create my own makeup just like you!" panted SWWNN.

"Oh, my god! That's wonderful! Let's compare!"

And with that Stevie led SWWNN to the small bathroom in between the two rooms. I sheepishly followed a few steps behind as Sciarra's eyeballs began to enlarge in their sockets.

I stood outside the bathroom as the women made themselves comfortable on the floor. Nicks then flipped the toilet seat cover down to turn it into a makeshift table as the two of them dumped the contents of their makeup bags onto it.

Stevie began, "The first thing I do when putting my makeup together is..." I was unable to hear the rest of the sentence as it was drowned out by the bubbling sound of Frankie's blood beginning to boil behind me.

In the hopes of getting their attention and perhaps breaking the flow of conversation to get things back on track, I leaned forward a bit into the room. The glare I received from the two of them for my impetuous intrusion caused me to stumble backward, retreating to the first room.

Frankie grabbed me by the collar and dragged me into a corner. Visions of a violent death before the dawn danced through my head.

He hissed, "I've got these fucking program directors here. Now get your fucking girlfriend out of there. NOW."

I walked back to the bathroom and gently knocked on the doorframe quietly saying, "Honey, there are some other folks out here who'd like to see Stevie."

Without looking up, Stevie called out in an annoyed tone, "WE'RE BUSY!"

Then she slammed the bathroom door in my face.

I. Was. Going. To. Die.

The mood in the room behind me was now turning ugly. The program directors used to being treated like their fecal matter had no odor were now staring down Frankie Sciarra, who looked apoplectic. The veins in his forehead protruded in an angry bulge that seemed to pulse with a Morse coded message of death for yours truly:

--. . - / -.-- --- ..- .-. / --. .. .-. .-.. ..-. .-. .-. .. .. -. -.. / - ..... / ..-.
..- -.-. -.- / --- ..- - / --- ..-. / - ..... .-. . / --- .-. / . .-.. ... . / - ..... /
-. . .-- / .--- . .-. ... . -.-- / ... - .- - . / - .-. --- --- .-. .. .-. ... / .-- ..
.-.. .-.. / ..-. .. -. -.. / -.-- --- ..- / .. -. / - ..... / - .-. ..- -. -.- / --- ..-.
/ .- / .-.. .- - . / -- --- -.. . .-.. / -.... ..- .. -.-. -.- / .- .-.. --- -. -. / .- /
.-. . ... - / ... - --- .--. / --- -. / - ..... / --. .- .-. -.. . -. / ... - .- - . / .--.
.- .-. -.- .-- .- -.-- .-.-.-

Which translates to, "Get your girlfriend the fuck out of there or else the New Jersey State Troopers will find you in the trunk of a late model Buick along a rest stop on the Garden State Parkway."

However, I now knew that death would find me as I had already tried and failed to break their discussion. I was doomed. There was no way I was going to open the bathroom door as Stevie would no doubt cast some horrible spell on me that would turn me into a newt or something even worse like an insurance salesman.

I thought, "Better death than life as an amphibious insurance seller."

So we waited.

Five minutes.

Ten minutes.

Twenty minutes.

Finally, the bathroom door opened. Stevie Nicks and SWWNN walked out arm in arm. They whispered to one another and laughed a private laugh as if they were childhood besties who'd finally gotten back together at a reunion.

Stevie said, "No one knows yet, but I've got a new album coming with Fleetwood Mac next year. We'll be back here to play, and I want to see you again."

They gave each other a final hug and then Stevie turned to the rest of us in the room.

"Good night, everybody!"

And she was gone.

She up and disappeared like a patchouli oil-scented fart in the wind.

Then the spell was broken. The program directors cursed out loud while steam burst from Sciarra's ears. I grabbed SWWNN by the sleeve of her Welsh witch blouse and dragged her out before I took one in the eyeball like Moe Greene's rubdown rubout in *The Godfather*.

Luckily, and somewhat surprisingly, I survived the night.

I don't remember how long it took before I had backbone enough to show my face around Frankie Sciarra again. It was probably several months, but at least I lived to tell the tale. The chance of actual physical danger to me was probably nil, but why risk it?

Flash ahead to the following year and the date October 28, 1987. As promised by Nicks, Fleetwood Mac had released a new album and came to play at the Spectrum. SWWNN and I were in the same backstage room again, though this time the circumstances were different. The room was crammed with dozens of people who had been given passes. One of them was WMMR's nighttime jock at the time, "Bubba" John Stevens. As the band's Christine McVie walked in the room he sighed, "I would drink her bathwater." My suppressed laughter forced a rope of snot from my nose, which I was demurely wiping from my upper lip, chin, shirt, jeans, and shoe tops when Stevie Nicks poked her head in from the hallway. The room hushed as Stevie surveyed the throng and scanned the room intently.

Her eyes came to rest on SWWNN, whom she pointed out to security.

"SHE can come back with me."

As SWWNN left me without a backward glance I let out a whimper.

While my girlfriend ignored it, Stevie took pity on my pathetic cry and snapped her thumb in my direction.

"Ugh. He can come too."

We then followed her back to her private dressing room. It was adorned with wall hangings, pillows, and throw rugs. It also had a bottle of wine the two of them quickly polished off while I stood, ignored, near the door.

I have little remembrance of what their conversation entailed. I honestly think it was just small talk and fan questions from SWWNN. As with many stars I've met, I think Stevie just craved a bit of honest conversation outside of the usual music industry hogwash.

SWWNN and I would part ways the following year, and I left Philadelphia shortly thereafter to further my career. While I never saw or heard from my evil ex again, I did cross paths with Stevie Nicks on a couple more occasions.

The first was when I returned to WMMR as fulltime host in the mid-1990s. Stevie had been friendly with DJ Ed Sciaky since she was a new, unknown artist. Ed, who'd been on the air since the early days of FM rock radio, had helped break her career open, as well as the careers of Bruce Springsteen and Billy Joel. Ed's show followed my own on Sunday afternoon and Stevie popped by to hang out and play records for a couple of hours. Of course, she didn't remember me, and I didn't bring up SWWNN, but it was nice to be in her special aura again.

I asked her what she was doing after the radio show that evening. She replied, "I'm taking my backup singers to the jewelry stores on Sansom Street here in town, and we're going to buy shiny things."

Naively, I told her the stores weren't open on Sunday.

She chuckled gently, saying, "Oh, they open for *me*."

I was a dope. Of course they opened for her. She was a famous rock star who made and spent a ton of dough, so they were delighted to open for her privately. Any day. Any time. However, I don't want you to think Stevie's attitude about it was haughty, it was just matter of fact. That's how life is for her.

She got that life by being both immensely talented and a very hard worker. I saw just how driven she is during our most recent meeting, which was in early 2018. I was tasked with interviewing band members for an impending Fleetwood Mac Channel on SiriusXM. Stevie would be available on a Sunday evening, so I took the Acela up that morning from Washington, DC, and met her at our studios early that night.

Stevie glided in with a small entourage dressed all in black. I noticed that she was not nearly as tall as I had remembered her as this was not a show day, so she had on flats and was really quite small.

As is the case with single-artist radio channels, the more recordings we have with the musicians, the better they are. It's just a lot cooler to hear the artist in between the songs explaining their music. I had no idea how much time Stevie was going to give but I was prepared with a stack of pages containing questions and lines for her to answer and read.

I asked how long we might be able to go.

She replied, "As long as it takes."

Stevie Nicks was relentless. We recorded for nearly four and a half hours. It was amazing. Some artists get bored or burn out after twenty or thirty minutes of doing this kind of stuff. Stevie realized the importance of her presence to the success of the channel so didn't let up.

At one point she asked what was next and I told her we would go down a list of Fleetwood Mac albums she was on. What I'd like from her was a few short recollections of making each particular record.

She said, "I can't do that."

I replied, "What do you mean? Don't you remember making them?

Stevie said, "Yes, I remember everything. That's why I can't give you short recollections. I either have to tell you everything, or else I can't tell you anything."

The woman wasn't joking. I would give her the name of an album and she would tell the story of her work on it from start to finish. Average answer time was close to twenty minutes. To put that in perspective, any other artist might give you twenty *seconds.*

It went so long and so well that we only got halfway through my list of wants for the channel audio. That didn't bother Stevie. She took the stack of paper and said she would finish the rest of the material at her home studio. And she did. She worked her ass off.

Before we parted for the night, she noticed a couple of tambourines tucked away in the corner of the studio. I'd brought them in the hope to have them signed but then didn't want to ask as we had gone so late.

Stevie quizzed me, "Are those for me to sign? Who are they for?"

I said one was for a family member and the other was for a musician friend, but it was far too late at night and I'd get them another time.

Stevie's manager shook her head and laughed sweetly, "She won't leave while there is anything she hasn't taken care of for fans."

I would have been happy with simple signatures. Not Stevie. She took *five minutes* to not only sign, but also inscribe and decorate the first tambourine. Seriously, it's a work of fucking art. She even embellished in between each of the cymbals along the side.

I said she needn't take any more time, but she did the second tambourine that was for Lzzy Hale. Stevie is one of Lzzy's main influences, and I knew she would cherish it as a gift. While it wasn't as ornate as the first one (her entourage and I were trying to get her to stop being so damned nice and taking so long) it still looked incredible.

On the way out she turned and gave me a hug, thanking me for working so hard and caring about her music. I gave her a little peck on the top of the head so I can now say I've smooched Stevie Nicks.

My experiences with her have shown me that you're never too big to not be nice to people and to continue to work hard even after you've supposedly made it.

Though it wasn't enough for me to ever again mention She Whom We Name Not. No tambourine for her.

But I'm not bitter.

THE TIME GENE SIMMONS OF KISS PROVED TO BE THE HOTTEST BOWLER IN THE LAND

As a misguided, rock 'n' roll loving lad, I was a member of the most-derided fan club in all of music history: the KISS Army. However, as I don't really give a shit whether KISS is cool or not to other people, I've retained my army rank through the years and return from my grease-paint-covered tours of duty with a real-life war story from the front lines of the rock wars.

First of all, we need to clear up a couple of misconceptions about KISS bassist Gene Simmons, and the band's music. Then I'll hit you with some personal KISS-related background, and then the story.

First of all, Gene Simmons is not an asshole. There. I said it.

Don't get me wrong. There is no greater wheeler-dealer in the rock world than Gene. I should know, the guy got a piece of every fucking quarter that passed through my hands in my early teenage years that didn't go into a pinball machine.

And he even got a lot of *those* quarters via the KISS pinball machines.

(SIDE NOTE: If this book actually sells and I make some money with it, the first thing I'm going to buy is a KISS pinball machine.)

Anyway, I don't fault Gene for wanting to make a ton of dough. He's honest about it. He's up-front about it. And when he has time, he's one of the nicest and most giving rock stars with fans, as this story will prove. He's not forcing anyone to buy anything from him. If it makes people happy, then let them buy all the fucking KISS merchandise that they want.

Besides, both Vinnie Paul and his brother "Dimebag" Darrell of Pantera were buried in KISS Kaskets. If KISS merch was good enough for the Abbott brothers to spend immortality in, then it's good enough for me.

The second misconception is that the music of KISS sucks. It doesn't. It's awesome. There. I said it.

Okay, I'll admit that it's not Beethoven. Unless it's the song "Great Expectations" from their landmark album, *Destroyer*, which is partially based on Ludwig van Beethoven's "Piano Sonata No. 8 in C minor." Other than that, it's not Beethoven. But much of it *is* brilliant pieces of insanely catchy pop metal.

And some people think I'm nuts when I say it, but I really believe that KISS is in many ways akin to another of my fave bands: The Ramones. Both groups started up in New York City at roughly the same time. Both bands were widely discounted for their music because of their style of dress. And, most importantly, both bands were mischaracterized for their music genres—punk for the Ramones, and heavy metal for KISS. They were really pop rock bands basing their sound on the great AM radio hits of the 1960s, which they all grew up on. Yeah, they both were later regarded as titans of their genres, but at their hearts were both doing short musical gems that should have been all over the radio.

My earliest awareness of KISS was in 1976 with the explosion of the *Alive!* album and its follow-up, the Bob Ezrin-produced *Destroyer*. I first glimpsed the *Destroyer* album cover art on a T-shirt at a boardwalk stand that summer in Point Pleasant, New Jersey. I thought Gene's dragon boots were the coolest things I'd ever seen. I was hooked and soon was listening to nothing but KISS on my Soundesign 8-track player. A couple of days before Halloween that year, I jealously guarded our family television against interlopers so I could watch the band perform three songs on *The Paul Lynde Halloween Special*. The show also featured Margaret Hamilton, the actress best known as the Wicked Witch of the West from *The Wizard of Oz* doing some Halloween shtick, as well as Florence "Mrs. Brady" Henderson singing a disco version of "That Old Black Magic." I can still hear the sound of my parents' eyeballs rolling behind me on the couch as I sat enraptured on the floor.

However, growing up as a "Hooligan" of "Flaming Youth" in a central New Jersey's "A World Without Heroes," the *Hotter Than Hell* "Rock and Roll Party" of Gene Simmons, the "Almost Human" "God of Thunder," seemed "100,000 Years" away from me getting to "Shout It Out Loud" as the "King of the Night Time World."

(Didja see what I did there?)

But in early 1977 my cousin Tommy and I somehow managed to come up with a pair of the toughest tickets to get on the planet: KISS at Madison Square Garden.

The band at this time was white hot, and KISSmania was at its peak around the world. As native New Yorkers, it seemed odd that they had never played the Garden before, but I later came to understand they purposely refused to play the venue until they could both headline and sell it out cleanly. The demand for tickets was beyond the beyond. So when Tommy called to tell me he'd scored a pair of tickets for the February 18, 1977, show on their "Rock & Roll Over Tour" at MSG, I would have been less surprised if he'd told me he'd come up with a pair of gold-plated hen's teeth from our grandmother's chicken farm.

That Sunday night in New York City is still burned into my brain. It ranks as one of the greatest evenings of my life. Plus, unlike my first concert at the Garden a couple of months earlier, I didn't vomit all over everyone. KISS had a small video crew there to capture the proceedings for posterity. It wasn't to be released—they would do a much more involved concert filming later that year at The Summit in Houston—but the band wanted a video record of their first performance at the biggest venue in their hometown. Once in awhile, I'll punch some of the grainy clips up on YouTube for fun.

While many of my fellow soldiers in the KISS Army outgrew the band, my love for them never abated, carrying over into my tenure at WHJY in Providence, Rhode Island. One of the first features I introduced when I arrived to do my show there in 1988 was "Kissin' Time." Named for one of their early songs, a cover of an old Bobby Rydell hit, it allowed me to play a string of KISS songs every Friday to help kick off the weekend. There was a huge population of KISS fans in Southern New England at this time, including the New England KISS Collector's Network, and they loved the feature so much the band caught wind of it. The group had never gotten a ton of love from radio, so the fans were really appreciative, and I believe the band was, too. They began to make sure I was always lined up for phone interviews and band press. They knew I was a fan and I honestly believe that meant something to them.

When KISS announced their Hot in the Shade Tour would play the Providence Civic Center on June 20, 1990, the whole city went apeshit. Rhode Island was not always a regular stop for bands, so with the group coming to town on the heels on one of their best albums in years, it was a big deal.

While doing my show one afternoon the week prior to the concert, the studio hotline lit up with a call. A deep, familiar voice spoke to me when I answered.

"Hello, this is Gene Simmons of KISS."

That's how every phone call I've ever had with Gene has begun. Doesn't matter who calls whom. It's always the same words.

"Hey, Gene! It's Lou. Good to hear your voice."

"I don't know if you're aware, but KISS is playing your city next week."

"Yeah, Gene. It's kind of a big deal."

He continued, "Well you might not know it, but I'll be in town the night before as it's an open day in our itinerary. I was calling to see if you wanted to hang out and do something together."

The fourteen-year-old KISS Army member in my head screeched at the invitation and then luckily passed out while my adult self was able to play it cool, saying, "That would be great, Gene. How about I get a car and I'll pick you up at the hotel when I get off the air that night at six?"

The plan was for me to get a limo and meet him and his bodyguard in the lobby. I also invited two fellow WHJY staff members, Chris Hermann and Sharon Schifino, to round out the party. Other than the time and place, we made no plans, figuring we'd wing it on the big night.

On the air that Tuesday afternoon, I just couldn't concentrate. My KISS addled brain raced at the thought of palling around town with one of my childhood heroes. At 6:00 p.m. that night the limo's wheels rolled up to the radio station, where Chris, Sharon, and I climbed inside and headed to the Biltmore.

Though it's been renovated and renamed since the time of our story, the Biltmore was the tip-top place to stay in Rhode Island. Built in 1922 and now on the United States Register of Historic Places, the hotel was gorgeous and boasted a great barroom that I loved to drink in. However, the building had never been cooler to my eyes than when I walked into the lobby that evening to see Gene Simmons and his bodyguard.

NOTE: My memory tells me that his bodyguard at the time was Andre Augustine. I've certainly dealt with Andre on many tours with KISS. He's a real gentleman, even if he is big and scary. However, as I check, it doesn't appear he was working with them until shortly after, but there was certainly a bodyguard.

I walked up to Gene and shook his hand. Even without his stage boots, he's a big guy.

"Hey, Gene!"

"Hello, Lou. I'm Gene Simmons from KISS."

"Yes, Gene. I remember." I then introduced him to Sharon...

"Hello, Sharon. I'm Gene Simmons from KISS."

And then on to Chris Hermann…

"Hello, Chris. I'm Gene Simmons from KISS."

With the introductions to the man who didn't need an introduction finally complete, I asked, "So, where do you want to go tonight?"

Gene replied, "I'd like to see some music. Are their any bands playing tonight?"

Sharon chimed in, "The only thing in town on Tuesday is the local band night at the Living Room."

Gene said, "Then let's go to the Living Room. Maybe we'll discover someone really good."

We then loaded up into the limo for the short drive over to the Living Room. Even though it was a bit beat up, it was the premiere rock club in Providence in 1990. The original version of the club ran from around 1975 to 1981, hosting an array of early punk pioneers before closing. The then current version of the venue had opened in 1982, and I loved the place. It was hot, dark, and nasty. I hosted many shows there including a few with The Ramones and a memorable gig with the Elvis Presley-impersonator-fronted, ska-style, Led Zeppelin cover band Dread Zeppelin. I still have Domino's Pizza boxes that had been delivered to the venue autographed by both The Ramones and Dread Zeppelin. I told you, I collect a lot of shit.

It being local band night, there were going to be dozens of local groups playing mini sets onstage, each hoping for their first shot at stardom. We all exited the limo and began the long walk from curbside up to the front door of the Living Room. Outside the club was a bevy of activity with dozens of musicians loading in or loading out their gear. Gene walked in front me, towering over everyone in

145

his body length black leather coat, and mass of long, black hair. As he glided past a kid loading his precious amplifier into the back of an old pickup truck, the amp slid out of the kid's hands and hit the ground almost as quickly as his jaw did.

"HOLY FUCK! IT'S GENE SIMMONS OF KISS!!!"

Now you have got to understand. "Local Band Night" is as tough a gig as there ever is in rock 'n' roll. It's meant to be a proving ground where you first get your feet wet. Many of the bands can be, I'll put this delicately, a bit *unpolished*. That's not a knock on anyone. If you wanna get your wings as a performer, the first step is usually at a local band night. It is exceedingly rare for anything really extraordinary to happen at one of these things.

That's why Gene Simmons sliding through the crowd outside the Living Room on a Tuesday night was enough to send a jolt through the crowd of budding musicians. In the meantime, our little group entered the club and wandered in different directions. Gene and his bodyguard walked toward the stage while Sharon stopped to chat with a friend. Chris and I made our way to the bar, where we each ordered a shot of Jack Daniels and raised our glasses to toast.

"Chris, we're actually out with Gene Simmons of KISS. This might be the best night of our lives!"

"WE GOTTA GO! NOW!"

It was Gene's bodyguard, who grabbed us just before we could down our precious bourbon shots.

"Too many people, time to leave!"

I looked over toward the stage, and there was Gene. Being so tall he was easy to spot. What made it even easier was that each one of the people in the crowd were pressed against him like drones around a queen bee. A fat tear rolled from my eye as I looked back at my forlorn shot of Jack, unquaffed at the bar, as I made my way to the door.

Safely back in the limo, I apologized to Gene.

"Sorry about that, Gene. Had I known it would get so crazy, I'd have suggested something else."

"Please don't apologize, Lou. It happens. I'm rather easy to spot in a crowd. I only hope I didn't seem rude by leaving so abruptly."

I then asked, "So what would you like to do now?"

The answer surprised me, and then puzzled me.

"I'd like to bowl. But I don't want PUSSY bowling, I want MAN'S bowling!!!"

I stared blankly for a moment and then asked the obvious.

Gene seemed a bit flustered by the question and didn't quite know how to explain.

"You know, Man's bowling. With manly pins and manly balls. Not pussy balls, MANLY BALLS!"

Now it was my turn to be a bit flustered. "Gene, I have no fucking clue what you're talking about."

Sharon saved the day saying, "Oh, you mean duckpin bowling!"

Gene erupted, "YES! THAT'S PUSSY BOWLING!!! I DON'T WANT DUCKPINS!!! I WANT MAN'S BOWLING!!!"

Being from New Jersey, where we all rolled with big balls, I was unfamiliar with duckpin bowling. It's more or less like regular bowling, but played with smaller balls and pins.

It was obvious that was NOT the style we'd be bowling that night.

If memory serves me correctly, the name of the alley we made our way to was The Cranston Bowl. Cranston was a nice working-class town on the southern border of Providence, and Sharon assured us the bowling there was great. When we first rolled up to the venue, I scurried inside and asked for the owner. An older gentleman came to the counter and I blurted out...

"Good evening, sir. Lou Brutus from WHJY radio. I have a VIP friend outside, and we'd like to come in and bowl, but we'd like a bit of privacy. I'll pay you any price you like, just give us a couple lanes at the far end of the alley. I will also be sure to plug you guys on the air big-time tomorrow afternoon!"

It's good to have a radio show sometimes.

The owner was cool as a cucumber. He scratched his chin and said, "Sure thing, Lou. We'll fix you up."

I returned to the car, gathered up the crew, and we made our way to our lanes. It was just a few minutes into the actual bowling that Sharon, Chris, and I came to a stunning realization.

Gene Simmons is one of the greatest bowlers in the history of the human race.

I am not fucking joking. Everything he threw was a strike. Not only that, he was doing it with trick shots. He was bowling between his legs, behind his back, and with double balls that would crisscross on their way to the pins. Gene threw strikes backward and forward. He threw one strike with his eyes closed.

Gene Simmons bowled the manliest balls any of us had ever seen.

During a break I finally asked, "Gene, how did you get so good at this?"

He answered, "Lou, I have been on the road for many, many years. I neither drink nor take drugs. THERE'S NOTHING ELSE TO DO OUT HERE. I don't mean to brag, but I'm also the greatest darts player you'll ever meet. I've also seen every major motion picture released in theaters since 1974."

His answer made total sense. Think about it. You're on the road for hundreds of days a year and there aren't a lot of choices, especially in some of the smaller cities. You can get wasted or sit around being bored, or you can get really, really good at something.

Gene chose bowling.

Our night of bowling went great. It also caused a wave of excitement in Cranston. Word quickly got out about our manly party and within an hour it looked like half the town was crowded into the bowling alley, keeping a respectful distance enforced by the kind staff of The Cranston Bowl. The owner graciously allowed us to bowl past their normal closing time, so it wasn't until much later that we were at the front counter saying goodnight.

I shook the owner's hand and thanked him for his kindness. I was very touched by his response.

"Lou, this is the greatest night we've ever had at the bowling alley."

Gene thanked him profusely and offered tickets to him and his staff for the concert the following night.

The owner declined, saying, "No, thank you, Gene. I'll be here at the alley. However, my granddaughter is your biggest fan, and she would be thrilled if you could sign an autograph for her."

Gene asked where she was and why she wasn't there. It turns out she was away at college at the University of New Hampshire.

"I'd be happy to sign something for her, but I'd love to speak with her as well. Can we call her up?"

The phone call was one of the nicest things I'd ever heard. "Hi, honey. It's grandpa. Sorry to wake you. No, no, everything is fine. You won't believe it though. Gene Simmons of KISS is here at the bowling alley and he wants to speak to you."

Her scream on the other end of the phone was audible to me across the counter. Gene then took over and chatted with her for the next ten or fifteen minutes.

It's one of my very favorite rock 'n' roll moments I've witnessed, and one of the reasons I believe Gene Simmons is a good guy. I've seen it other times at shows and out in public. If he has time, he will chat and sign and take selfies and do all he can to make fans happy. He does this all the time. However, if he doesn't have time, he will say so. Gene isn't mean, he's just blunt. If he can do it, he'll do it. If he can't, he'll tell you flat out.

I've had many interviews and interactions with Gene through the years. He chose my radio show in Chicago to first announce the KISS reunion tour with Ace and Peter. It was also my pleasure to help put together the KISS channel on SiriusXM in 2019 ahead of their "End of the Road" tour, spending two days with the band at their rehearsal space in Hollywood. I still bring him a stack of stuff whenever I see him, and he and the rest of KISS are always good about signing it.

Even after all these years, I still get a thrill to see KISS in concert, and I always get a chill when I think back to that night at Madison Square Garden with my cousin Tommy in 1977.

I supposed at heart I'm still a fourteen-year-old KISS Army member.

And there's nothing UNMANLY about that!

THE TIME FRANK ZAPPA MADE
MY HAWAIIAN SHIRT FAMOUS

I'VE ALWAYS BELIEVED FRANK Zappa to be one of the musical greats of the twentieth century. Probably the best of all. His penchant for howlingly funny lyrics often overshadowed his genius as a composer and an arranger as well as his spot-on commentary regarding society. In person he had a great sense of humor and was brutally honest. I'm fairly certain Frank Zappa was the smartest man I ever met, though I'm not smart enough to know for sure.

He's also the only human being who could have made an ugly Hawaiian shirt of mine known throughout the Western world.

Well, at least amongst Zappa fans.

I first began listening to FZ in my early teenage years. As with any other guys my age all I could think about was sex, so I naturally gravitated toward dirtier Zappa ditties like "Dinah-Moe Humm" with its hilarious narrative of off-the-wall sex with the title character. I later discovered his live album with The Mothers, *Fillmore East–June 1971*. That record is chiefly made up of a song cycle featuring singers Flo and Eddie taking on the characters of a rock star and a groupie. Featured songs included the size-of-my-member classic "Bwana Dik" as well as the condom-wrapped musical majesty of "Latex Solar Beef." This record might be the best example in history of something NSFW: Not Safe for Work.

I initially saw Zappa in person on Friday night, October 27, 1978. The concert took place during his annual string of Halloween shows in New York City from the mid-1970s into the early 1980s. These performances, done for many years at the aging Palladium theatre where my first FZ show was, were insane, filled with costumed concertgoers who had a reputation for being the weirdest group of human beings assembled anywhere on the planet. Truly demented folks. Frank brought that out in people. They *wanted* to be weird for him. It's why you went. Then there was the band. It was the best musicianship I'd ever seen. And it wasn't like these guys were doing bar band versions of "Louie, Louie." They were playing challenging music with intense arrangements and were expected to follow Frank's visual and vocal cues that could instruct everything to change gear in an instant. Plus, it was all fucking hilarious. Our show featured an old standby bit that Zappa did in-concert called "The Dance Contest." In an audience filled with whack-a-doodles, he would find the absolute craziest among them to bring onstage, where he would interview them like a demented game show host before tasking them with the entertainment of the audience via their dance moves.

One dance contest I witnessed, I believe in '79 though it might have been that gig in '78, was more memorable than most. One fellow pulled from the stew of human bizarreness, dubbed "The Dynamic Butch" by Frank, looked and acted like he had a head full of acid and a pants load of live salamanders. The sequence with Butch and the others that night was so freakish it was included as "Dance Contest" on Zappa's *Tinsel Town Rebellion* album released in May of 1981.

Using an ever-changing array of breathtakingly talented musicians, Zappa regularly toured until the end of 1984, after which he took himself off the road with no rock concert performances at all in 1985. At this time, I was in my second year working as a morning show producer and weekend air talent at WMMR in Philadelphia. It was one of the few rock stations of the time that dared to play Zappa's music. We also celebrated greatly when he came to town so were a known quantity to him. As October 1985 came closer on the calendar, the station's general manager Mike Craven approached me with a surprising question regarding the Halloween season. He wanted to know what Frank Zappa was doing for the holiday that year.

Now you have to understand that Mike was not a rock 'n' roll kinda guy. I don't mean that as an insult, it just wasn't his nature or job. He was the chief suit for the radio station, the guy in charge who reported to the corporate weenies who owned the parent company. It was his job to keep the coffers flowing with loot from the advertising. Mike had a great sense of what made WMMR successful and that meant usually not sticking his nose into programming matters. He was smart enough to not fuck with a goose that laid golden eggs.

That's why the exchange surprised me.

"Hey, what are our plans for Halloween this year?"

"I'm not sure yet, Mike," I replied.

He asked, "Isn't that the big holiday for Frank Zappa?"

"Yes, but he's not touring this year, so there's nothing on his schedule."

"Well, you're a big fan. Why don't you call him up and invite him to spend Halloween with us in Philadelphia? We can turn it into a big party."

It was a genius idea. A number of us from the morning show and the promotions department then put together a plan. We would turn the annual radio station Halloween party into a Frank-themed event dubbed "Zappaween." There would be Zappa music, an FZ lookalike contest, and Frank himself could be the judge of the costume competition.

All we needed was Frank Zappa.

Managing to track down his home phone number, I called Frank's house and got his wife Gail on the line. It was she who oversaw much of Frank's business and I would have to win her over for this to happen. I needn't have worried. She loved the idea of the party, and Frank was excited as well because he was apparently bummed out that he had no Halloween plans for the first time in several years.

At first I was concerned that Frank might want a large talent fee for coming out to host the shindig. However, Gail had very few requests for the appearance, which included both the party and a couple hours in the studio with us live on the morning show on Halloween. She ran down the list with me over the phone.

"We'll need first class roundtrip airfare for Frank from LA to Philly."

"Done."

"Frank would like to stay at the Four Seasons while in town."

"Of course."

"And when he comes in to do the morning show, he'd like an espresso machine."

You see, Frank partook in neither drugs nor alcohol, but the man drank black coffee like a fiend. It's how he had the energy to release sixty-two albums during his lifetime with over forty releasing after his death. The cat was fucking wired on caffeine from the time he rose each day in late afternoon till he went off to bed at dawn.

"Gail, we will have an espresso machine waiting on Halloween morning."

The party planning was a blast. We'd hold the event at the swanky Adams Mark Hotel. Admission would be free but you'd have to win your tickets from the radio station. Zappa fans from around the world went apey trying to get ahold of a pair. People were going to fly in from every corner of the globe just to watch Frank judge Halloween costumes. Zappa lookalikes and soundalikes began contacting us at the radio station. The insane weirdness from his Halloween concerts would carry over to the party for sure. It was as exciting as looking forward to an actual concert.

As for the espresso machine, we went the extra mile. We spoke with the folks at the Adams Mark Hotel about our need and they offered us one of their machines along with a coffee steward. No shit. A fucking coffee *steward*. Long before Starbucks baristas fueled the world's coffee addiction, this hotel had guys dressed in general's uniforms whose job it was to custom-make caffeinated beverages so strong that meth heads would have run off to rehab after half a cup with a bad case of the shakes. And the machine itself was a marvel of engineering. It was humongous, needing three men to carry it into the studio to set up.

When Zappa walked into the studio that morning, the first thing he saw was the machine and his personal coffee steward.

He got a big ol' smile and Halloween was off to a great start. As Frank's outspoken social and political commentary had made him a target of threats, his bodyguard Chuck Ash accompanied him. Now there's an interesting guy. At the time, Chuck was a Pennsylvania state trooper as well as the mayor of his hometown on the outskirts of the city, Phoenixville, Pennsylvania. Prior to that he had been in the military going back to the 1960s, with several special duties tours of Vietnam as a young man. Surprisingly, he was a huge fan of Frank's and the two of them were friendly for years.

The morning show appearance went well and the party that night was a hoot. Frank wore no costume himself, showing up in dark suit and tie. I was dressed as a priest, and as we were both raised as good Catholic boys, we got some funny shots of me kneeling before him in prayer while Frank leaned toward with me a cupped ear to hear my "confession."

The entire event went so well we all agreed to do it again the following year.

The Zappaween party for 1986 was to be held at the Trocadero in Philadelphia's Chinatown. It was an old theatre that had recently been refurbished by a local promoter and turned into a live music rock club. The party would follow the same format as the previous year, so it should be a breeze.

This is where Hawaiian shirts enter the story. Halloween fell on a Friday that year and we had a running gag on the show that the end of the workweek was "Hawaiian Shirt Gonzo Friday." The idea was to wear the loudest Hawaiian shirt you could find to celebrate the weekend kickoff. It was silly, perhaps even stupid, but people really liked it. I did, too. Plus, these were the days where you could still find classic old shirts from the fifties and sixties in thrift stores.

That's why when Zappa walked in the studio that morning we were all wearing shirts so loud you'd swear that each one had a wireless volume control. During a commercial break I asked Frank if he'd like us to rustle him up a costume to wear that night."

"No thanks, Lou. But I'd love it if you could find me a really ugly Hawaiian shirt to wear tonight."

"Frank, I'll make it happen."

And I did.

Before the party that night I went back to my apartment to change into my costume and to pick out a shirt from my personal collection of vintage Hawaiian monstrosities for Frank. The shirt I chose was a hideous mix of purple with pink orchids and gold leaves. It looked like Pele, Hawaiian goddess of volcanoes, had vomited the contents of an entire beachside pig roast in a searing lava of digestive juices.

It was pretty fucking ugly.

On the collar of the shirt I stuck a matching gold pin that was a map of the state of Montana, a nod to Frank's song "Montana," which was all about becoming a dental floss tycoon. No, really.

As for myself, I was dressing as Frank from the cover of his *Sheik Yerbouti* album. I'd rented an Arab sheik costume and purchased a fake mustache and beard that perfectly matched FZ on the album cover.

When I met up with him before the party, I gave Frank the shirt and told him he was welcome to it keep as a gift. He laughed as he came out wearing it.

"I'm in your clothes and you're in mine. We're dressed as each other for Halloween!"

The Zappaween party that year was another smashing success. To be honest, it was personally some of the most fun I ever had in my life. It's not often that one of your heroes dresses as you for Halloween. Our staff photographer Mike Johnson shot a great photo of Frank and I together. It remains my favorite image I've ever gotten with an artist. I was sad that we weren't able to do it again for 1987, but Frank had made other plans and was gearing up to return to the road. I then left WMMR in January of 1988 to move on with my career.

However, the story doesn't end there.

It was in April of 1988 that Frank was to release an entire album of live guitar solos simply entitled *Guitar*. I anxiously waited for release day and headed off to the record store that morning. Yes, places where you could buy physical music product in-person existed everywhere in those days. What I found when I arrived first shocked and then delighted me. I went to the "Frank Zappa" section of the CDs and began going through all of the albums trying to find the new one. This took a little a while as Frank had so many fucking albums his section was the biggest in the store. Finally, I found a cover I didn't recognize. Sure enough, the word "Guitar" was scrawled in Frank's handwriting as well as his name along the top. A stage shot of FZ from the chest up adorned the cover, his face a mask of concentration staring down at the neck of the guitar obviously playing a solo.

Then I noticed something else. Something wonderful. He was wearing a shirt. An ugly Hawaiian shirt. My shirt.

"HOLY SHIT! MY SHIRT!" I yelled, and scared the living piss out of everyone in the store.

A clerk ran over from the cash register. He probably thought my shirt had caught fire. As he came up to me, I stuck the CD cover in his face.

"FRANK ZAPPA IS WEARING MY HAWAIIAN SHIRT!"

"You should probably leave now, sir."

"LOOK! LOOK! LOOK! MY HAWAIIAN SHIRT IS FAMOUS!"

"You should *definitely* leave now, sir."

I took the disc to the register, paid for it, and then went to record store after record store to buy any other copies I could find. While most anyone I mentioned the story to stared back at me with looks of torpid disinterest, my fellow Zappa-loving friends were duly impressed with my shirt's new position in the world.

However, the shirt wasn't done yet. Apparently, Frank really liked the damn thing and wore it on the cover of magazines as well as the cover of a cassette tape release from "Guitar World."

Through the years, I kept in touch with Frank and Gail. I even got to visit their home up in the Hollywood Hills where Frank would play me whatever new releases he had coming down the pike. On one trip, I recall us eating pepper steak at 3:00 a.m. while we sat on the couch in his downstairs studio complex listening to what would be his "You Can't Do That Onstage Anymore" series direct from the multi-track tapes. For a kid who grew up worshipping the guy, it was a pretty awesome way to spend the night. As always, he was honest and straightforward and fascinating to listen to.

I saw him live whenever I could and caught several shows on Frank's final tour in 1988, including his last live performance in the United States. That show with opener Hot Tuna was held at Nassau Coliseum on Long Island on March 25. Then in 1990 Frank was diagnosed with terminal prostate cancer. He'd apparently had the disease unnoticed for quite some time, and it now was inoperable. However, he was able to fight off the disease for couple of years, and I was excited when I learned that he would be appearing in Europe in September 1992 with a German classical group called Ensemble Modern. They were going to present live selections of Frank's classical music during stops in their hometown of Frankfurt, Germany, as well as Berlin and Vienna. Frank was advertised as the emcee for the night, and it was rumored he would perform with and or conduct the group.

I looked at my meager savings account and decided I was going to take every cent I had in the world to fly to Europe for a stop on the short tour. Originally, I wanted to go to Berlin as I'd been there for Roger Waters's performance of the "The Wall" at the Berlin Wall in 1990 and loved the city. Then I thought I should go someplace I'd never been so should travel to Vienna. However, my finances were so shaky that I ended up going to the tour openers in Frankfurt, as it was the cheapest. This turned out to be a fortuitous turn of events.

Before the trip, I reached out to Gail as well as Frank's publicist. I jokingly told them that I was to be the sole representative of rock radio in the United States. Sadly, that actually turned out to be true. They were both happy to hear I was coming, inviting me to the rehearsals and sound checks each day. I kept quiet and out of the way with my little yellow stage pass dangling from my neck, tip-toeing around Frankfurt's beautiful Old Opera House that was originally built in 1880. I still have the pass! Frank had a large lounge chair on stage for rehearsals, as he was in a weakened state.

There were to be three performances in Frankfurt, and I was going to catch all of them. On the first night Frank took part in the opening as well as closing the show by conducting the encore of "G-Spot Tornado." Sadly, he was feeling too ill to make the second night and then appeared only briefly the third show. It was my last time seeing him. He was feeling so sick that he was unable to travel for the other performances in Berlin and Vienna, choosing instead to return home. It gave me a grim bit of happiness to have ended up in Frankfurt due to my poor finances.

I cried for several days when Frank passed away in December of 1993. By then I was back as a fulltime DJ at WMMR, working the late-night shift. For a week after his death I did thirty- to sixty-minute blocks of Zappa music every night as a tribute.

I saw Gail only once after Frank's death. It was a concert at the Stone Pony in Asbury Park, New Jersey, with the band Z. The group featured Dweezil and Ahmet, the sons of she and Frank. I should have reached out to her more, but it was just too difficult for me to do, and I had absolutely no idea how to talk to her about her loss.

As for my Hawaiian shirt, I never learned of its fate. After Gail's death in October of 2015, a family estate sale was put together and took place in November of 2016. There were hundreds of musical instruments, pieces of recording equipment, and memorabilia, as well as personal artifacts including clothing. I combed every piece of the online catalog before the auction but saw no sign of my shirt. Then in late 2019, just as we were wrapping up this book, an image of Frank wearing the shirt was used for an archival vinyl release entitled *The Guitar World According to Frank Zappa*. I laughed out loud when I saw it.

It may now be lost to history but for a short time my Hawaiian shirt shone like a white-hot star of sartorial ugliness at the very center of the musical universe.

THE TIME A PAIR OF DAVE MATTHEWS BAND TICKETS HELPED ME TO LEARN SENSITIVE MILITARY INFORMATION INSIDE THE SITUATION ROOM OF THE WHITE HOUSE

IT WAS IN EARLY 1999 that I stumbled upon an impending military action that would shake the corridors of power around the globe. I learned about it with the assistance of a pair of concert tickets.

In 1998 and 1999, I was hosting the morning show at WHFS in Washington, DC. I hated the job. It was a poorly run operation coasting on the appeal of its once-a-year HFStival concert. I couldn't wait to get out of there and was not surprised when, after decades as a rock station, they later folded up and flipped formats to Spanish-language dance music.

However, while I was there, it did put me in contact with some interesting, non-music-industry folks. The first thing I noticed was the large amount of request line calls I received from people who were unable to say their names or where they worked. Many of these were employees of secret-keeping places, like the Central Intelligence Agency or the

National Security Administration. Some of the NSA callers had a subtle way of letting me know where they were...

ME: Where are you from?

CALLER: Someplace where I don't have a Furby.

ME: Ahhhhh, understood.

Furbies were small, furry toys in the 1990s that kids could talk to. The toys recorded voices and also used early face-recognition technology to assist in carrying on conversations with the child. Because of the danger of them being used to record sensitive information they were banned inside of the National Security Administration.

During the impeachment of President Clinton, I received a call from one of the pages in the US Senate who listened to me each day. He invited me to watch the opening of the impeachment hearings from the Senate gallery. I ended up attending several days of the proceedings, including the historic final vote. While I was allowed to speak about attending, I wasn't allowed to identify the fellow who gave me access, so I referred to him on the air as "Mister X." This was a wise decision, as my presence in the gallery did not go unnoticed. I was told that Peter Jennings of ABC News threw a fit as I was regularly in the gallery while only two out of the three network newscasters were allowed at any one time. "Mister X" was the son of a prominent senator, and when the morning of the final vote came, I was hidden in the senator's office and locked in. Shortly before the vote, they hustled me upstairs to the hallway outside the Senate gallery. The place was jumping with journalists and Washingtonians attempting to get in for this incredible moment of history. I was told to stand with two or three other "friends of the pages" near the door and wait for the word. Seconds before the gallery was sealed, a page inside nodded at my guy outside. We were then rushed into the gallery to take the final empty seats. The vote itself only took a few minutes, but it was exciting to be there.

So it wasn't a total surprise to get a request line call one morning in early March of 1999 from someone who said, "Forget about that Senate junk. How'd you like to get in for a private tour of the White House?"

Turns out the fellow on the line handled something related to the hiring of military security for the Clinton White House. He didn't go into too much detail, and I figured it was the kind of thing I shouldn't ask about. We exchanged personal information and I called him at his office after I got off the air. He would need the names of anyone coming with me, and there would have to be security checks on everyone involved.

In a tip of the cap to Deep Throat, the codename for the insider who fed information to the *Washington Post* during the Watergate scandal of the 1970s that sank the Nixon administration, I referred to my White House connection over the air as Sore Throat.

The following weekend I was standing with a few family members outside the Old Executive Office Building in Washington, DC. This is where the office of the Vice President is located, among other things, and it's where we began our tour. Sore Throat took us around there before we moved over to the nearby White House, where things really began to get interesting.

And by "interesting," I mean "kind of disappointing." At least at first.

The first thing I noticed about the West Wing of the White House is that it's kind of...shabby. That's because it's essentially an office that is used twenty-four hours a day, seven days a week, so everything is a little beat-up. I was stoked to see the 1906 Nobel Peace Prize that Teddy Roosevelt received for brokering the end of the Russo-Japanese War. The following day, I made the mistake of mentioning on the radio where it was placed in the room. This led to an immediate call to my studio hotline from Sore Throat, who let me know in no uncertain terms that I could not publically mention where specific items are in the White House as it was a security risk.

The tour was instructive, but not terribly eventful. I was allowed to take pictures in the pressroom, but the rest of the White House was off-limits for photography. As it was a Sunday morning, things were pretty quiet, and the uniformed Secret Service officers eyed us blankly as we walked around. We were taken to the Oval Office and our host pointed out the famous "windowless corridor" where Bill Clinton received the official presidential hummer from Monica Lewinsky, which helped lead to his impeachment. The Secret Service officer in that area rolled his eyes at me as I chuckled.

At one point, our host was going to take us upstairs to see the apartments where the president actually lived with his family. The flag indicating the presence of the president was not flying over the White House that day, so "Sore Throat" assumed we were cool to go up. As he placed his foot on the first stair, the Secret Service officer seated there looked over and laughed, "Where do you think you're going?"

Our guy replied, "Upstairs. The flag's not up."

"Well, they're home!"

Needless to say, we didn't go up. However, I'd have loved to run into Bill Clinton. Sore Throat explained that the president sometimes walked around the White House looking for regular folks to speak to. He'd quiz them about where they were from and could rattle off facts about wherever it turned out to be. Apparently he knew the name of damn near anyone in politics anywhere in the country.

As we were about to wrap up the tour, Sore Throat pointed to a sealed door with a prominent RESTRICTED AREA sign on it. He explained that this was the White House Situation Room and that access to that area was extremely limited. I mentioned I was familiar with its history going back to the Kennedy Administration, and I was bummed out I couldn't see it. That's when Sore Throat picked up a nearby phone and began a conversation with some unknown person.

"Hello, it's me. I've got Lou Brutus from WHFS out here and he wants to look at the room. Can we let him and his family in?

He paused for a moment then turned to me and asked, "Is the Dave Matthews Band playing in town later this year?"

"Yes," I replied, "And I'd be HAPPY to get you and any of your staff and friends into the show!"

KA-CHUNG! The door of the Situation Room unlocked and we walked in.

The fellow I assumed Sore Throat had spoken to stood there in uniform. I shook his hand and introduced my family members. Then I looked around.

There wasn't much to see. The Situation Room of the White House was kind of old and overused. This was before its 2006 renovation that brought it into the modern age. The first things in particular I noticed were the long conference table in the middle of the room and a white phone with a golden presidential seal on it.

"Is that one of the phones I can launch missiles from?" I laughed as I jokingly reached to pick up the receiver.

The two of them spoke in unison, "DON'T. TOUCH. IT."

I didn't touch it.

Then I looked up on the wall, and just like in some John Grisham film, there was a row of clocks with different times on each one. I read the city locations out loud from the nameplates beneath each clock.

"Washington, DC, Tokyo. London. Kosovo. Kosovo? Hey, guys, isn't there some crazy shit rumored to be happening there soon?"

The two White House men looked at each other and then back at me.

"You didn't see that. You've never seen it. It doesn't exist. It will never be discussed. This is not the sort of thing you should wish to talk about on the radio. Ever."

At this point it was time to leave.

The airstrikes from NATO began on March 24, 1999, and continued to June 10.

The Dave Matthews Band played Bristow, Virginia, on August 1, 1999.

I thought it best to stay far away from both.

THE TIME I WAS PEED ON BY A FAMOUS
ROCK 'N' ROLL DOG

A WISE MAN ONCE said, "It is better to be pissed off than to be pissed on." I can vouch for the truth in that statement.

In February of 2018 I was to hit the road with the space-themed band Starset. Hailing from Columbus, Ohio, they're known for their technologically forward-thinking song lyrics, electronic-leaning music, and stage show that looks like a science fiction film come to life. The front man is Dustin Bates, who appears during their performances—known to fans as "demonstrations"—dressed like a scientist or lab technician. The other members of the group—Ron DeChant, Brock Richards, and Adam Gilbert—are dressed in space suits including full helmets. They wear jetpacks that shoot smoke, the drums disappear before your eyes inside of a specially designed plexiglass cube, and the tour I was to travel with would also have an augmented reality feature where attendees using a free app would be able to see objects flying around the concert hall while viewing the band through their phones. Very entertaining and groundbreaking stuff that I was excited to see.

The plan was to join up with the tour in Milwaukee, Wisconsin, then travel overnight for the gig in Rockford, Illinois, and then up to Fargo, North Dakota, for a third show before flying home. The band had given me an open invitation to join them on the road and I'd picked out these particular dates as they both fell on a weekend and allowed me to get to North Dakota, where I had never been before. Of course, traveling to North Dakota, where icicles can form on a man's taint in mere seconds while relieving himself out of doors, in the middle of February probably wasn't the brightest idea I've ever had. A smarter fellow would have gone on tour down south with some other band that time of year, but I was excited to see the stage show and cross one more state off my list for seeing all fifty.

I flew into Milwaukee's Mitchell Airport the Friday morning of their gig in town. Being a military history buff, I'm always happy to see the World War II Mitchell bomber at the entrance, imagining myself as some kind of rock soldier coming in on some sort of musical commando raid. I went from the airport right to the venue where the band's tour bus sat silently in the empty parking lot. I tiptoed onboard. The group was still sleeping while I was already wired on black coffee, so I grabbed my cameras for a quick trip to the city's lakefront to shoot pictures of nearby lighthouses. I'm kind of a lighthouse nerd and was glad to get images of three in the area, including the North Point Lighthouse, the Milwaukee Breakwater Lighthouse, and the Milwaukee Pierhead Lighthouse. I then Lyft-ed back to the concert hall, where the band was now up and moving.

When I climbed back onboard the tour bus, I was greeted by Dustin Bates, who was holding a little furry friend. It was Ernie, a tiny French bulldog just a few months old whom Dustin had recently acquired and brought on the road. Ernie was so small you could hold his whole body in your two cupped hands. Naturally, I couldn't wait to take him into my arms.

One thing you should know is that I adore animals. I believe that the love and companionship they bring us are one of the greatest gifts we receive in life. Along with the gift of gab, I've also been lucky enough that most animals, even usually standoffish ones, like me. I tend to enjoy their company better than that of other people. The one thing I hate about going on the road is that I get homesick, or as I call it "puppy sick," for my Darla the Wonder Dog.

So it is with these thoughts that I immediately reached out to take Ernie. I cooed as I took his furry body into my hands, stared into his bulging puppy eyes, and said, "Oh, Ernie. You and I are going to be the best of friends!"

That's when Ernie pissed right down the font of my photographer's vest.

Being a small dog, I quickly deduced that most of Ernie's body must have been made up of bladder because the torrent of urine that sprang forth from his puny puppy penis was not unlike those statues you see in Europe of cherubs endlessly whizzing into a fountain. It didn't end until my vest appeared to have been used as a flotation device after a forced water landing by a passenger airplane in the Yellow Sea.

Ernie gave me a stare as if to say, "This is my bus, Radio Boy. I run this joint, and if you don't want more of the same then you'd better not fuck with Ernie! Now scratch my ass and make me a sammich!"

Dustin was more contrite. His initial reaction was, "ERNIE, DUDE!" He then helped pat me dry and we took Ernie outside. On return to the bus, Ernie positioned himself on the top step of the entryway, like Gandalf defending the bridge against the balrog in Lord of Rings, and barked at me saying, "YOU SHALL NOT PASS!"

It was gonna be a long tour.

However, my usual knack with animals began to kick in and Ernie warmed up to me. As I sat in the front lounge of the bus doing some social messaging about the trip, Ernie scurried around my feet, chewing on my sneaker laces, all the while huffing and puffing like a terrible beast.

That's when I dubbed him Ernie the Wicked Pup.

The name began to stick online and my listeners fawned over images of Ernie. The Starset fans were already very familiar with him and howled at the first-ever use of the Instagram hashtag #ErniePeedOnMe.

However, among the band members, unbeknownst to me until later, he was known as Silent But Ernie. This was because, much like his ability to create endless geysers of puppy pee, Ernie's tiny hindquarters gave birth to a putrid parade of silent-but-deadly farts. This is not a joke. That little ragamuffin let loose with stinkers so bad I begged our tour bus driver to stop so I could get out one of the space helmets to use as a World War I gas mask. The paint was peeled off the wall in the bunk where Ernie slept. His ass had been banned in four states. Death would come swiftly to those who breathed too deeply of the fearsome flatulence of his noxious nethers. You can actually find him on Instagram at @SilentButErnie. No shit. Except the smell.

Of course, band guys being band guys, Dustin thought it would be height of hilarity to have Ernie sleep with me in my bunk so I'd get a snootful of his vehemently vesicatory vapors on my first night. Luckily, I caught wind of the plot (no pun intended) and escaped the lungful of anal puppy death.

But even after all that, Ernie and I became pals over the course of that long weekend through the frozen wasteland of the upper Midwest. In the frigid temperatures the only thing to keep me warm in my pee-stained vest was his super-heated farts. Their constant humming sound lulled me to sleep.

When it was time for me to head to the airport in Fargo and leave the tour in the wee hours that Monday, Ernie climbed into my vest, curled up, and went to sleep. When I nudged him awake, he looked up with sad eyes as if to say, "Don't go, Lou." I told him that I'd miss him, but I had to get home to my Darla. He then told me I was a good guy and a friend to all animals.

Then he let loose with one last fart, so hot and foul that it burned the hairs out of my nostrils.

THE TIME A BAND OF MUSICAL SUPERHEROES DRESSED ME UP AS A LOBSTER THEN BEAT ME UP IN FRONT OF A THOUSAND PEOPLE

WHEN ASKED ABOUT MY job, I often say, "I'm a professional music fan." It seems a pretty apt description. I'm just a music fan who went pro. I suppose you might also say I'm a professional audience member as I spend so much of my waking time as part of a crowd viewing a show of some kind. Outside of working as an emcee at concerts, I'm not normally onstage that much. However, on one steamy night of rock 'n' roll, I did become part of the show...and got more than I bargained for.

It was June of 2006, and I was in my fifth year at XM Satellite Radio. This was prior to the later merge with SiriusXM. One of the channels I oversaw at the time was the punk rock offering called Fungus 53. It played a little of everything from the entire genre, including pop punk, hardcore, and ska punk. It was a fun channel to program, and I got to deal with an interesting array of characters from the punk world.

One of the most imaginative and colorful from the ska punk part of the genre was The Aquabats. To describe them as just ska punk actually does them a disservice. They mixed together ska, punk, new wave, classic rock, and surf rock. However, the thing that set really set them apart was that they performed in matching superhero outfits and claimed to have been the product of an outlaw scientist's lab experiments. The zaniness of their appearance sometimes blinded people to the fact that the band, which in their early days featured a full brass section, was an absolute powerhouse. As a matter of fact, one of their early drummers was Travis Barker of Blink-182, who began his career as Baron von Tito with The Aquabats.

Plus, as you might imagine, they were really, really, really funny.

Some of my favorite songs from the group included "With Cat with 2 Heads," "Powdered Milk Man," and "Fashion Zombies." One thing that got lost in the sauce with all of the wacky music is that everything they performed was G-rated. Absolutely clean with no cusswords or sex. It's just it was so weird that some people just assumed it wasn't for everyone.

The live show was especially nuts with the group often battling costumed villains onstage, sometimes being assisted by audience members, many of whom were parents with young kids. One thing I loved was "The Kid Toss." That's where lead singer Chris Jacobs, aka M. C. Bat Commander, would take a kid out of the crowd, pick them up from under their armpits, and then fling the kid as high and far over the audience as he could. And you'd be surprised at how far you can toss a kid! It was the audience's job to safely catch the kid then surf them back to mom and dad.

Being a big fan, and having seen and interviewed them numerous times, I was hoping to catch them playing songs from their then recent album *Charge!* When I saw they would be in Washington, DC, performing near our studios, I invited them in for a live broadcast. The radio concert was a hoot and the band kindly invited me to their gig that night at a club called Nation.

When I entered the dressing room, both the Bat Commander and another founding member, guitarist "Crash" McLarson, greeted me warmly. As they autographed a poster for the show that night along with two-paper plates they had used to write out their set list for the radio show that day, the Bat Commander made me an offer I couldn't refuse.

"How would you like to appear onstage tonight with The Aquabats?"

"Wow, that would great! What would I be doing?"

"We'll put you in a giant lobster costume then bring you onstage so the crowd can boo you and then we'll have a big battle while the song plays. Are you in or you out?"

"I'm in."

Who could turn down an offer like that? It seemed like it would be easy to do and a ton of fun. What could possibly be hard about it?

Plenty.

First of all, it was June in our nation's capital. Very hot, and very humid. The club was packed with people and it was so moist you could actually see the air. Son, it was nasty in there. And that was *before* I put on the giant lobster outfit. After I wriggled into it on the side of the stage about halfway through the set, it covered about three quarters of my body. My cam shorts, milky white legs, and sneakers showed out the bottom.

"YOU LOOK GREAT, LOU!!!"

I think it was Crash McLarson who shouted to me over the music after ducking offstage, but I couldn't tell because there was very little in the way of vision inside that lobster shell. And even less breathable air. It was so hot I was making my own lobster bisque inside. The sweat ran down the crack of my ass and onto my sack, where my nuts were now shrinking into my body at the thought of blindly going onstage dressed like the Gorton Fisherman's nightmare.

"GET READY, LOU!!!" I heard a member of the stage crew off to my side yell, who then positioned me to make my entrance.

I then heard the Bat Commander from the stage where the music had stopped.

"ARE YOU KIDS HAVING FUN?!?!?!"

<Rapturous cheers>

"WELL, ME AND THE AQUABATS ARE HAVING FUN, TOO!!! BUT THE FUN MIGHT BE OVER BECAUSE WE'VE JUST BEEN TOLD AN EVIL VILLAIN HAS ARRIVED WHO'S HERE TO STOP US FROM HAVING FUN!!!

<Jeering begins>

"HERE HE IS, KIDS, THE VILLAIN WE WERE WARNED ABOUT...THE ROCK LOBSTER!!!"

The road crew then shoved me onstage to a chorus of boos so loud you'd think that Yoko Ono had just walked out to brag that, yes, she did indeed break up The Beatles and you could all wank yourselves for the trouble.

"BOOOOOOO!!! BOIL THE LOBSTER!!! BOIL THE LOBSTER!!!"

For a bunch of kids and mutant ska fans, they seemed a rather ruthless lot.

The Bat Commander then continued...

"WELL, KIDS. THE AQUABATS ARE GONNA PLAY A SONG NOW AND WHILE WE DO, WE'RE GONNA TRY TO DEFEAT THE ROCK LOBSTER, BUT WE'LL NEED YOUR HELP, SO MAKE A LOT OF NOISE!!!"

The crowd erupted, the band kicked back into gear, and I started to get the living shit kicked out of me. No joke, they were beating me like a red-shelled stepchild. The way the guys had described it to me earlier made me assume it would be super easy and not violent at all.

I was very, very wrong.

The Aquabats pummeled me from every direction. They whaled on the head and body of my lobster self. I quickly lost my bearings inside the suit and did my best to hold my claws up in a pitiful act of oceanic self-defense. The crowed cheered with a fevered bloodlust of hatred for all crustaceans. For the first minute or so, the only light was from the stars that I saw each time a particularly vicious blow landed on my head.

Suddenly, the suit lined up so I could see. There was the sanctuary of the side stage, if only I could make it! I stumbled in that direction, and just as I was about to cross over to safety, a roadie blocked my way, grabbed me by the shoulders shouting, "WHERE DO YOU THINK YOU'RE GOING?!?!?" He then shoved me back toward the superhero-costume-clad musical fiends.

I don't know how long the battle went on, but it seemed like a long time. I finally collapsed onstage to the delight of the crowd and the Bat Commander declared victory.

"WE'VE DEFEATED THE ROCK LOBSTER, KIDS!!! THANKS FOR YOUR HELP!!!"

I was then dragged corpselike from the stage, fully expecting to meet my final doom in the catering area in a giant pot of boiling water and melted butter.

After the set was done, the guys low-fived me as my body ached too much to raise my arms for high-fives and congratulated me on my performance. I think I had lasted longer than other guest lobsters at previous shows. I shall update my résumé with this tidbit.

The Aquabats still tour and continue to do their "Aquabats Supershow." I last caught them in the summer of 2019 and we had a good laugh about my lobster adventure—especially when I told them I was including the story in this book. Chris Jacobs, the Bat Commander, also went on to be one of the creators of the hit children's show *Yo Gabba Gabba*. They remain a tremendously creative unit and are still the only group I'd dress up as edible seafood for.

THE TIME DAVE GROHL PROVED HIMSELF THE MOST DOWN-TO-EARTH ROCK STAR ON THE PLANET

TO BE HONEST, MOST people I've met in the rock 'n' roll world, including many of the big stars, have been fairly down-to-earth people. I suppose it's because in a lot of cases the assholes weed themselves out. Making it in the music or broadcast industries is tough enough and having to deal with someone who's a shithead makes it tougher, so people do their best to jettison those who bring too much toxicity. The flip side of the coin is that some people have so much coolness seeping out of their pores that they're a fucking blast to be around at all times. Dave Grohl is one of those people.

I first saw Grohl the one and only time (I think) I caught Nirvana in concert, which was at Club Babyhead in Providence, Rhode Island, in September of 1991. I also (very vaguely) remember (very drunkenly) seeing Nirvana at J. C. Dobbs in Philly in 1989, but I can't be sure. Either way, they were loud, loose, and really intense. Other than that, I don't remember too much from the performance, as I was wasted and trying to bang one of the barmaids (to no avail).

However, I've seen Dave Grohl plenty of times with Foo Fighters, both headlining shows and as part of the bill at some big festivals. The strangest appearance among those, though, was at the Live Earth benefit concert at Wembley Stadium in London in July of 2007. It wasn't that their music wasn't great. It was. Their short set was on fire and the UK crowd was more intense in Foo-natical devotion than any audience I'd ever seen in the US. It's just that they appeared in between sets by The Pussycat Dolls and Madonna, which was disconcerting to my concerted concert concentration.

That was also the same day I got shitfaced with Spinal Tap's "Stonehenge" dwarfs, but that's a story for another time.

The story I wanna tell you about was a Foo Fighters festival appearance in Baltimore, Maryland, on May 14, 2005. The gig was at the stadium home of the Baltimore Ravens and also featured performances by alt-bands like They Might Be Giants, Garbage, Interpol, Echo & the Bunnymen, Billy Idol, Social Distortion, and Good Charlotte. I arrived early to record an interview with Grohl and his band mate, the always charming and funny Taylor Hawkins.

As happens normally at these big events, the band had a long list of press to do before they could even think about their actual performance. Things can go a bit crazy as the artists dutifully do their best to tackle their many appointments, usually aided by a small army of assistants, record company personnel, management employees, tour overseers, and various others. Some bands have ginormous entourages while baby bands might have to handle most everything themselves. Foo Fighters that day had a relatively small amount of folks to help steer them through their tasks.

PRO TIP: Be on time! Don't ever be late or you won't be invited back to do anything with that artist, which is in addition to the fact you won't get your interview that day. It's rule number one!

Right on time, I met up with the band in some nondescript concrete room on the main floor of the stadium. However, as soon as I walked in there was a flurry of discussion among the management/tour/record company folks, and it was decided we could not possibly use that room for interviews. The couple of other folks who would be doing interviews and I were told we were all going up to some pressroom several floors above us in the stadium. The whole group—including the band, band helpers, and interviewers—started hustling to the elevator.

A few moments later the entire crowd of us, easily twelve to fifteen people, were at the door of one of the stadium elevators.

I pushed the UP button and we all waited.

And waited.

And waited.

As often happens at these stadium extravaganzas, the elevators were being used overtime. With so many people going to so many places, it was obviously tied up somewhere above us.

The army of assistants then all leapt into action. Every one of them pulled out their phone or a walkie-talkie or both and began trying to outdo one another in attempts to get the band to where they were going.

"WE NEED A FOO FIGHTERS ELEVATOR NOW!!!"

"FOR GOD'S SAKE, THE BAND IS HAVING TO WAIT FOR AN ELEVATOR!!! WE NEED ASSISTANCE NOW!!! DO YOU HEAR ME??? NOW!!!"

"EITHER GET ME AN ELEVATOR OR GET A GOLF CART HERE TO DRIVE THE BAND UP THE RAMPS, BUT THAT WILL BE THROUGH THE CROWD SO I'LL NEED EXTRA SECURITY!!!"

And on and on and on. If this much attention and intensity is ever turned to the problem of world hunger, I can assure you every starving child on the planet would be obese inside of a month.

In the middle of all the shouting and posturing, Dave Grohl—calm, cool, and unperturbed—looked at the still lit elevator UP arrow and shrugged his shoulders. He then walked over about ten feet to his left to the door marked STAIRS. He opened the door and looked up, asking, "Why can't we just take the stairs?"

He then ran up the two flights of stairs to our pressroom. No meltdown. No shouting. No diva drama. Just a bit of common sense.

Good ol' Dave Grohl.

THE TIME I LEARNED THE HORRIBLE TRUTH
ABOUT HEAVY METAL FEET

SURE, BEING IN A touring rock 'n' roll band sounds like one of the most glamorous gigs on the planet. You may think it's all travel, booze, drugs, and unbridled sex. But there is only one thing you can truly count on when hitting the road: the smell of feet.

And that's the terrible truth of the whole music biz. The stuff you look forward to isn't all it's cracked up to be while the last things you would ever want are what you get every day. Yes, you'll travel, but it will grind you down. Yes, there'll be booze and drugs, but if you overdo them, they'll burn you out or kill you. Yes, there *might* be sex, but the chances of picking up an unpronounceable disease are very high.

The smell of feet is the only thing in rock 'n' roll touring that actually comes as advertised.

I learned my horrendous lesson at day one of the 2008 edition of the Rock on the Range in Columbus, Ohio. As in every other year the festival was held, I interviewed a ton of rockers, including Disturbed, Stone Temple Pilots,

Staind, Killswitch Engage, Shinedown, and a bunch more of America's finest hard rock bands. However, it was a group of Australians who taught me what was afoot with feet.

The band was Airbourne, a hellbent-for-volume group led by the brothers Ryan and Joel O'Keeffe, who owed at least a bit of their sound to fellow Aussies AC/DC. That year during the concert, they were playing second stage. As with some of the other up-and-coming bands, they didn't have the dough to travel by bus and so were barnstorming America in a giant van.

Now lemme tell ya, other than doing a tour in your own car, which sometimes does happen, there is nothing more grueling than a van tour. Actually, a van tour is probably worse. When artists travel by car, it's often solo acts. If it's just you with maybe one or two other people, it can be relatively comfortable. When a band with a crew travels by van, it means you've got up to a dozen sweaty rockers crammed in like sardines.

And sardines smell better.

Because if you're rolling in a van, it normally means you're not making a lot of cash. Without that extra money, you don't have the financial power to get hotels, which leads to everyone sometimes going up to a week without showering. Put those unwashed bodies all together in a tightly packed van along with a week's worth of dirty laundry, crumpled fast food bags, and grungy, toe-jammed sneakers, and you have a recipe for really wretched redolence.

This is all why you don't normally wanna conduct an interview inside of a band's van. It's also usually so crammed with stuff (clothes, gear, cases of water, etc.) that there's no room anyway. But on this day, as the band didn't have a dressing room and everywhere around the stadium was getting the full brunt of music from the stage, it was deemed necessary for Airbourne's singer Joel O'Keeffe and I to record in the van.

Initially, I wasn't too worried. Most interviews at these big festivals tend to be on the shorter side. Both the bands and the radio rats like myself have too much scheduled, so we tend to agree to do quick chats of ten to fifteen minutes. I figured, "How bad could it be in that van for ten minutes?"

The answer was *plenty fucking bad.*

The first hint that my nostrils would soon be a proving ground for the kind of stink not normally enjoyed outside of a sweaty ass crack several hours removed from a refried bean feast was just before Joel unlocked and opened the door. The van had windows all around and as I looked through the glass it seemed the air inside shimmered. "That's odd," I thought. "It's not hot enough for the heat to build up and get wavy like the air over blacktop in the summer. Why does it look so strange?"

The answer was foot odor.

As the unwitting lead singer opened the van door, not only was my sense of smell summarily slammed by the aforementioned mingle-mangle of malodorous odors, but also by a hitherto unknown fragrance of feet so frighteningly foul that the appallingly putrid, podiatric permutation caused my sinuses to burn as if I was a mustard gas victim at Ypres, Belgium, in World War I.

However, Joel seemed oblivious to the smell, no doubt having built up a tolerance to it like the mutant creatures who live in the Exclusion Zone around the radioactive wasteland of Chernobyl, so I had no choice but to hold my breath and follow him into the van.

It seemed a cruel irony that a band called Airbourne could launch such an assault of airborne nastiness. As I settled into the vehicle, I thought that only a group of Australians could produce a smell so akin to a rancid outback nightmare, vile vapors from the hindquarters of some lactose intolerant beast force-fed whole milk on the gibber plains of the Great Victoria Desert. It was like dingo farts of death wishing me a chipper "g'day, mate!" I tried not to breathe through my nose, taking only short, shallow gulps of air with my mouth while preparing my deck to record our conversation.

"Hello, I'm Lou Brutus speaking to you from Rock on the Range in Columbus, Ohio. My guest now is lead singer of Australia's own Airbourne, Joel O'Keeffe. Thanks for joining me."

"Thanks, Lou. Great to be here!"

Unfortunately, my first sentences had used up the entire supply of air I had inside my lungs and before I could ask a follow up question, I took a breath.

Oh, the horror!

The stench caused the bile to rise from my esophagus and the acid of it burned the back of my throat. I felt a blackout coming on so willed myself to blurt out one last sentence.

"Thank you, sir. Joel O'Keefe of Airbourne has been my guest!"

Then I clutched at the door handle, flung open the van, and fell face first to the pavement.

"What the fuck, mate?" I heard Joel's voice from above and behind me.

I gasped for air by way of an answer.

When I gathered my wits and stood up again, I felt a sharp edge with my tongue and realized I had chipped one of my lower teeth during my face plant. Embarrassed, I apologized to Joel and told him the van smell had overwhelmed me. He laughed, saying, "That's the smell of rock 'n' roll, mate. You'd never make it in a band." He then graciously allowed me to reconduct the interview, this time outside the van. The music from the stage was loud, but at least it didn't smell.

For the record, most tour buses and all tour vans have some kind of smell going on—I'm not just dogging on Airbourne. And it sometimes seems the odor problem is more of a guy thing than a girl thing. For example, when you go to the back of In This Moment's tour bus, you enter the private domain of their singer Maria Brink. It smells like fresh-baked cookies. However, not all women who tour with a bunch of guys in a rock band have it so good. I believe it was Emma Anzai, bassist for the group Sick Puppies, who told me, "My bus stinks of boys."

So let this story be a cautionary tale to you if you wish to answer the clarion call of rock 'n' roll. Even if you practice hard enough to not stink when you play, you still might stink.

THE TIME I ACCIDENTALLY BECAME A ROCK STAR AS WELL AS THE MOST HATED MAN IN THE STATE OF MICHIGAN

THIS STORY SHOULD BE its own book. It should be a movie. It should be taught in schools as a lesson on how you can't believe a fucking thing that you see or hear in the media. It is the unlikeliest tale you will read in these pages, but I assure you that every word is true.

First, a bit of backstory. When I was working in Chicago in the late 1990s, one of the groups I struck up a friendship with was Watershed. They're a phenomenal, straight-up rock band, very much in a Cheap Trick vein, out of Columbus, Ohio. They released an album entitled *Twister* on Epic Records and Jo "Mama" Robinson, our music director at the radio station as well as a Columbus native herself, introduced me to the group and their music. I immediately hit it off with the members, bassist/singer Joe Oestreich, guitarist/singer Colin Gawel, and drummer Herb Schupp.

Over the course of the next several years I kept in touch with the guys, mostly Joe and Colin, while also showing up at as many gigs as I could. We loved many of the same bands—especially Cheap Trick—and baseball, too. However, the most important thing they introduced me to was Buckeyes football at THE Ohio State University.

Of course, I knew about the Buckeyes, but being from New Jersey, I didn't know how rabid their fan base actually was. As fate would have it, I ended up in Columbus one Saturday during college football season. I don't remember the reason, though I suspect I was there to cover some tour. Anyway, I was out with Joe and Colin and couldn't help but notice it seemed like kind of a ghost town. I thought that odd, as this was a bustling Big 10 college city.

The guys said matter-of-factly, "The Bucks are on."

Apparently, as the Ohio State Buckeyes were playing an away game, the entire city was glued to their sets. I don't mean "some" of the town, and I don't mean "most" of the town. I mean every man, woman, and child other than us was watching the game. I think we were on our way to a studio, where we would have the game on while everyone worked. The deserted streets looked like a scene from Charlton Heston's *The Omega Man*. The few people we did see greeted us by calling out with the traditional Buckeyes cheer, "O! H!" To which Joe and Colin answered correctly with "I! O!" The whole of the population was totally in tune with the football team.

As I spoke with Colin and Joe about OSU's football history, the subject of "The Rivalry" came up. This was the matchup each year against the Michigan Wolverines. It was traditionally the last game of the season and went all the way back to 1897. To give you an idea how heated the rivalry was between these two bordering states, in 2000 ESPN did an end of the century list of the ten greatest rivalries in sports.

The Red Sox versus the Yankees was number seven, the Maple Leafs versus the Canadiens was number five. What was number one on the list?

Ohio State versus Michigan.

When I discussed the Michigan Wolverines with Watershed members or other Buckeyes fans, their eyes would narrow and they would speak with disgust in their voices. I mean they fucking hated Michigan. Not in a funny "rah-rah" kind of way; they wanted to exterminate everyone from "that state up north" like roaches. It wasn't just a football thing; it was some kind of insane xenophobic obsession.

The whole subject really piqued my interest. I'd never seen such raw emotion for anything in sports. I don't know why, but I became fixated on the rivalry, and it crowded out other thoughts. I read up on its long history, including the two most famous coaches to face off against one another in the series, Woody Hayes of Ohio State and Bo Schembechler of Michigan.

One day while I was out walking, I began sing-songing some lyrics to the cadence of my footsteps. Much like the "Hey! Ho! Let's Go!" from The Ramones' "Blitzkrieg Bop," I began to sing out "O! H! I! O!" That made me chuckle a bit, but then thought that in true punk rock fashion, it should be edgier, so I began to throw in the first name of former Michigan coach Schembechler, "Hey! Ho! Fuck Bo! Hey! Ho! Fuck Bo!"

Now that sounded like something Ohio State fans would take notice of!

I finished up the lyrics, but as more songs based in the world of the OSU versus Michigan rivalry came to me, I began to wonder what band would actually do songs like this.

Thus was born the legend of The Dead Schembechlers.

The name was an obvious nod to one of the favorite punk bands of my youth, Dead Kennedys. I started to dream up the concept of a punker group that existed only as a musical vehicle of hatred toward the Michigan Wolverines. I had written many silly tunes and parody songs for the radio show, but I was now on a mission to write as many punk tunes inspired by the rivalry, the nastier the better.

The lyrics came fast and furiously for songs like "Michigan Stadium Is a Pile of Shit," "Ann Arbor Girls Are Dirty Whores," and "I Wipe My Ass with Wolverine Fur." I had the melodies in my head with everything sounding like the first wave punk bands I grew up loving like The Clash, The Ramones, Johnny Thunders, Buzzcocks, and others, including the aforementioned Dead Kennedys.

Not only that, I created an entire alternate history for the band. They'd supposedly been around for years, only performing on the eve of the rivalry game against Michigan, the show referred to as "The Hate Michigan Rally," playing to tiny crowds while dressed like late OSU coach Woody Hayes. Group members would wear matching black pants, white short-sleeved button-down shirts, black clip-on ties, red windbreakers, and classic block "O" baseball caps. Oh, and the old 1950s-styled horn-rimmed glasses.

Finally, the fake band history included long passages on how everything bad on the planet was the result of the International Wolverine Conspiracy. Researching every famous U of M grad I could find, I tied them into a nefarious plot to take control of the planet and set up a New Wolverine Order. It included everyone: political commentator Anne Coulter, former vice-president Gerald Ford, and even Ann B. Davis, the actress who played Alice on *The Brady Bunch*.

I called up Colin and Joe and told them about the whole thing. Their response was immediate.

"Get on the next plane to Columbus. We're gonna record those songs."

Each band member would have the first name of Bo, while also getting a famous punk rock last name and persona. Colin would be drug-addled guitarist Bo Thunders, Joe would be mute but violent bassist Bo Vicious, while I was to be group singer and mouthpiece Bo Biafra. As Watershed's then current drummer Dave Masica was unavailable due to back surgery, we enlisted Mike Sammons of the band Twin Cam to be drummer Bo Scabies.

It was the summer of 2004 when I arrived back in Columbus and went directly to a basement studio in the home of band friend and sometime Watershed member Mark "Poochie" Borror. The songs came quickly as we all had great musical frame of references from our many years of hanging out. As there was no pressure attached to this, we were only doing it for fun, we laughed throughout the sessions at the wonderful stupidity of the whole thing.

At some point during the recordings, one of the studio crew looked at me and said, "A band based on the rivalry. Why didn't anyone think of this before?"

I answered, "'Cause you guys take this shit waaaay too seriously."

He solemnly nodded in agreement.

We took a few hours off one day to gather up our Woody Hayes costumes and go take band pictures outside of the Ohio State stadium, lovingly known as "The Horseshoe." Poochie turned the tracks around quickly and I had my artist friend Alan MacBain create a band logo for us. The logo, inspired by that of The Ramones, featured a bird skeleton holding a majorette's baton and buckeye leaf while its mouth contained a banner that read "Hey, Ho, Fuck Bo." I then ordered a couple hundred CDs to be released under the title "Rocket to Ann Arbor" on the made-up music label Flaming Wolverine Death Records, and we made plans to do a gig that November.

Now you need to understand, no one had any belief that anyone anywhere was going to take any notice of this. We did all of it solely for our own amusement, and I feel I speak for everyone involved when I say creating all this was some of the most fun I ever had in my life.

Two weeks before what was actually our first gig, no one outside of those who had worked on the record had ever heard of The Dead Schembechlers before. It was a figment of my imagination, laced with a handful of songs, a few promo pictures, and a MySpace page. So Colin reached out to two close friends at the local indie rock station CD-101: program director Andyman and DJ Brian Phillips. We let them in on the plot and they agreed to not only sponsor The Hate Michigan Rally, to be headlined by Watershed with the "triumphant return" of The Dead Schembechlers as opener, they also came right on board with the idea of presenting the fake history of the band as real. The entire staff, especially Brian, did an astounding job of selling the story that we'd been around since 1990, had fought the National Guard during the band-led "High Street Riots of '96," and that this would be a chance for many to see our "legendary" band for the first time inside the city limits since then.

The entire world, including the press in both Ohio and Michigan, bought the entire bullshit story, hook, line, and OSU team-colored sinker. We were dumbstruck. I flew into town the day before the gig and we quickly rehearsed our set, which would be made up of songs from our album along with my character ranting and raving like a pigskin-crazed, anti-Michigan Mussolini. The buzz on us around the city was incredible and it looked like the gig would sell out before show time. The local music papers had picked up on the story with some blurbs, and I'd done several newspaper interviews. CD-101 was hammering our songs every hour, and we even received requests from local sports reporters to cover the show. There were numerous references to us as "The Best Damn Punk Band in the Land," a bastardization of the Ohio State's "Best Damn Band in the Land."

However, on the morning of the gig, we realized just how nutty things had gotten.

I was awoken by a phone call from Colin. He was so excited I couldn't quite understand what he was saying. Finally, it began to sink in what he was on about. That morning we were on the front page of the biggest newspaper in the state of Michigan, the *Detroit Free Press*. I don't mean a blurb; I mean there was a huge, above-the-fold photo of the band under the banner headline "OSU PUNKS RIP MICHIGAN RIVALS." Not only that, we were the top item of discussion on sports radio in both states and our songs were being played on radio stations in both of the competing fandoms.

We had hit the big time.

The gig that night at Little Brother's on High Street in Columbus was a powder keg. The line for the show went around the block. Our drummer, Mike Sammons, unrecognized in street clothes, walked along the waiting crowd outside listening to the comments.

"I can't believe I'm actually going to get to see the legendary Dead Schembechlers."

"My brother was there with them when they lit a couch on fire during The High Street Riots."

"I heard the International Wolverine Conspiracy had threatened to assassinate them, but they're still gonna play"

All these folks were utterly convinced we'd been around since 1990. The press helped this along. I suppose nobody thought to factcheck a band of guys dressed like a deceased football coach, and they printed everything I claimed in the interviews unchallenged.

When the time came for our set, Brian Phillips rang out with our carefully scripted introduction.

"LADIES AND GENTLEMEN, BOYS AND GIRLS, BUCKEYES OF ALL AGES! WILL YOU PLEASE WELCOME, FROM THE MUDDY BANKS OF THE OLENTANGY, THE BEST DAMN PUNK BAND IN THE LAND! FLAMING WOLVERINE DEATH RECORDING ARTISTS, THE LEGENDARY DEAD SCHEMBECHLERS!!!"

A bloodthirsty cheer went up and then we started to kick the sold-out crowd's ass.

You gotta understand, the guys playing onstage with me are incredible, national-touring musicians. Joe, Colin, and Mike sounded like a punk rock buzz saw as we dove into our opening number, the pseudo-autobiographical "Dead Schembechlers."

We took an oath, we swore in blood

On a stormy winter night

To keep Ohio from the grasp

Of the evil Michiganites

Join us now, comrades in arm

And wear the scarlet red

We won't give up till kingdom come

And the Wolverines are dead

Dead Schembechlers

Dead Schembechlers

Dead Schembechlers

Yeah!

Though the song was unknown to anyone just a couple of weeks prior, the crowd was shouting the lyrics back to me from the start. The set passed by in the blink of an eye.

I was an honest-to-god rock star.

Joe Oestreich took me to the game the following day and we watched as the Buckeyes upset the favored Wolverines. The highlight for me from the game was watching the crowd react to the Buckeye's band doing "Script Ohio" where they spelled out the state's name in cursive, ending with the dotting of the letter "i." Tears streamed down the faces of thousands around me. It was like being at a religious service.

I began to more fully understand why our band had struck a chord.

The game was back up in Michigan the following year, but we booked a show in Columbus anyway. This time, however, Dead Schembechlers would headline with Watershed as main support. I also spoke to my friends in the swamp rock band from Louisiana, Dash Rip Rock, who agreed to play a set as "musical representatives of the Southeastern Conference who also hate Michigan."

Finally, there was a fourth band on the bill added as a way of heading off musicians in Michigan who were trying to challenge us. After our initial success the previous year, we'd been contacted by several Michigan musicians who claimed to be the "North's answer to the Dead Schembechlers." At first, we considered inviting one of them to play the festival. Then I thought, "Fuck those guys. We'll be like professional wrestling. We'll control both the heroes AND the villains!"

That's how The Dropkick Woodys were born.

I quickly pulled together a few musicians I knew in the DC area and got them into a local studio to record a couple of pro-Wolverine songs I'd written. The first was "I Spit on Woody's Grave" and the second was "Buck the Fuckeyes."

We hurriedly put out a press release regarding the songs and made them available online. The Michigan fans took notice and were soon heralding The Dropkick Woodys as "The Defenders of the Maize in Blue." Interview requests from the press soon followed. In some cases, I would be talking to a reporter one day as Bo Biafra of The Dead Schembechlers then the following day as Dropkick Woodys leader Brutus Schmuckeye. They printed everything.

At the beginning of 2006, the third year of our actual existence and sixteenth year of supposed existence, there was a great amount of anticipation. Both Ohio State and Michigan were expected to vie for a national championship, which meant the game that year, to be hosted in Columbus, might be of gigantic importance in the history of the rivalry.

Everyone in the band decided we must go balls-out all year on The Dead Schembechlers. We reconvened in the studio to record several new songs including one that became one of our biggest, a musical hit piece on Michigan's quarterback entitled "Chad Henne Is a Motherfucking Joke." It was the last song we did in the sessions and was just thrown together as a barroom sing-along with clapping hands and clinking glasses. This made such an impression that years later when Henne played for the Miami Dolphins, opposing defensive players would scream the lyrics to him across the line of scrimmage...

Chad Henne is a joke

A motherfucking joke

His Wolverines are gonna fucking croak

They call him Doctor Choke

Bet on him and you'll go broke

Cause Chad Henne is a motherfucking joke

Our other "hit" from these sessions was "Bomb Ann Arbor Now," a hard-rocking look at a nuclear first strike on the University of Michigan. To help promote it, I cobbled together a video using old atomic bomb test footage from the 1940s, and it quickly topped over 200,000 views on YouTube.

However, the masterstroke for the Hate Michigan Rally's success that year was Joe and Colin's insistence that we book the Newport Music Hall on High Street ourselves. This was the big room in town with a capacity of 1,700, and the gamble was that the game would be so big that year that we could lure Buckeyes fans into the show for us to sell a ton of merch and turn a handsome profit.

As the season progressed, both the Buckeyes and Wolverines racked up victories. Week after week, it appeared that this year's game between them in Columbus would be of huge importance to the national championship picture.

The only hiccup in things was when our namesake, former Michigan football coach and then current athletic director Bo Schembechler, had a health scare. He'd had a long history of heart disease, which led to the formation of the Bo Schembechler Heart of a Champion Research Fund. Bo was taken to the hospital a couple of weeks before our game, but thankfully turned out to be fine.

It was during his return to work that he got a visit to his office by John Niyo, a sportswriter for *Detroit News*, who later told me the whole story. During the interview they conducted, John asked a fateful question.

"Bo, have you ever heard of The Dead Schembechlers?"

Schembechler replied, "What the hell is that?"

"They're a rock band from Columbus. They dress like Woody Hayes and they sing songs about how you and the Wolverines suck."

"I don't believe it!"

So then Niyo opened up our website to show it to Bo. He was incredulous.

"My god, it's true! They do dress like Woody." He perused our site, reading the lyrics and checking out the pictures. Then he looked up at his son who was in the room and said in a triumphant tone, "See? I still fucking matter in Columbus!"

Bo wasn't mad at our band, he was elated with us. We embodied everything Wolverine fans detested about Ohio State fans, and we'd made him Public Enemy Number One.

Soon after, both Michigan and Ohio State played their final games before the season-ending rivalry contest, and something occurred that had never before. Ohio State and Michigan were not only both unbeaten, they were #1 and #2 in the national rankings.

It was going to be the biggest game in the history of The Rivalry.

When game week arrived, we'd heard that the Ohio State coaches and players had been instructed not to say a word about us. We were seen as so foul, offensive, and hostile that it would be a public relations nightmare to even acknowledge us.

But Bo Schembechler didn't give a hoot in hell about making OSU look bad and he made us famous around the world.

As the face of Michigan sports more so than the Wolverine football coach at the time Lloyd Carr, Bo was brought out at the beginning of the week to address a gymnasium full of reporters. They were all chomping at the bit to ask about his health, the team's game preparations, and his thoughts on what would be the biggest day ever in The Game. But it was Bo who got in the first question. In front of the cream of the sporting press from around the world, he asked, "Have any of you ever heard of the Dead Schembechlers?"

BOOM.

In the blink of an eye, we went from a footnote in this century-long rivalry to front-page news around the world. While the game continued as the main story, we became the secondary tale for a football-hungry public. We ended up as part of the game coverage in the *New York Times, Los Angeles Times, Boston Globe, Sports Illustrated, Seattle Times, Austin American Statesman*, and countless other publications. Full cover pictures of us were used for both hometown arts papers *U Weekly* and *Columbus Alive*. Fox News and various ESPN shows were reporting on us with Sport's Center quoting our song lyrics around the clock.

We had hit pay dirt.

As the week rolled on and the story of the group got bigger and bigger, things actually began to get a bit scary. Reporters were snooping around the homes of the other guys in the band, death threats were coming in from Wolverine fans, and even some Ohio State supporters were claiming our obscene lyrics brought disgrace on the state.

I was staying in Columbus with Joe and his wife Kate. The plan on show day was for us all to get into our Woody Hayes outfits at his house then drive over the Newport Music Hall, where we'd scheduled a press conference in the late afternoon. Not only were all of the sporting press coming, we'd also received a request from HBO, who were in town filming for an upcoming documentary.

For that brief moment in time, those precious few hours, we were the hottest rock band on the planet. I don't mean that we were as big as the Rolling Stones, Guns 'N' Roses, or Metallica. It's just that on that one day there was no other group on Earth generating as much press, interest, or outrage as The Dead Schembechlers.

We chuckled as we readied ourselves to leave and dreamed of the money we'd make selling out the show and selling off every last scrap of merch we had. It was gonna be a payday!

And that's when the entire thing blew up in our faces.

As we walked toward the door, I called out to the other band members to hold up. I wanted one last look at my email, this was pre-smart phone days, just in case any last-minute press requests came in. I saw an email from reporter John Niyo. I opened it and my stomach sank as I read it.

BO SCHEMBECHLER JUST COLLAPSED ON THE SET OF HIS TV SHOW IN MICHIGAN. VERY BAD. GET READY.

Oh, shit.

We ran to the TV set and put on ESPN. The report had just come in.

Bo Schembechler, press benefactor and namesake of our group The *Dead* Schembechlers, had just died.

We were fucked.

I don't mean just regular fucked. I mean we were fucked worse than any band in the history of rock 'n' roll had ever been fucked. In a nanosecond, we had gone from a hilarious band of loveable misfits to a group of musical lepers living a nightmarish *Twilight Zone* existence.

What the fuck were we gonna do?

My first instinct was to tell the guys we couldn't do the show. We'd have to cancel, but that raised other points.

"The promoter could sue us."

"The fans might riot."

"What happened to 'the show must go on?'"

That last one hit home. We'd made our filthy pigskin bed and now we'd have to lie in it like a muddy sty.

It was Joe who said, "Listen, we gotta play. They're not going to cancel The Game and we shouldn't cancel The Hate Michigan Rally. It's not about money. Fuck the money, we'll give it to Bo's charity, but we gotta play the gig."

I called my dad in New Jersey, himself only a month from passing away due to cancer, and explained our predicament.

He whistled, "You're in a tough spot."

When I told him of Joe's idea to play the show, but give all of the band's money from it to the Bo Schembechler Heart of a Champion Research Fund, he said, "I think you've found your way out."

So we got into the van and headed to the hall for our press conference. On the way over, our phones were all exploding. I didn't answer mine, but Colin picked his up. Someone told him that Rush Limbaugh had been on the air saying that the game and our show had to go on. I still don't know if he actually did say that, but it didn't matter. We were now in some bizzaro world where anything could happen.

Our press conference, which originally was going to be a fun-filled rant on how the Bucks would stomp the Wolverines and how best to battle The International Wolverine Conspiracy, was instead a solemn affair. I made a brief statement about how Ohioans both loved and hated Bo, he was a native of Ohio as well as a former OSU assistant coach to Woody, and that nothing our music ever did could take away from his legacy. We then ignored any questions from the press and filed back to our dressing room. Some of the photographers asked to get pictures of our merchandise so they could get the words "DEAD SCHEMBECHLERS" on camera, but we thought they sounded like vultures and we didn't bring out anything to sell the whole night. It would have been blood money.

In the meantime, the marquee above the entrance of the theatre changed the lettering from HATE MICHIGAN RALLY to GOD BLESS BO. The fans dutifully lined up outside and waited to get in for what promised to be one of the most bizarre nights of music the city had ever seen.

Watershed opened the gig and the crowd began to loosen up. I paced backstage trying to think of what I should or shouldn't say during the course of the gig. We all decided that we'd have to address Bo's death, though we wouldn't change any lyrics save for one. I insisted that instead of singing "Hey! Ho! Fuck Bo!" during "Buckeye Bop," we substitute "O! H! I! O!" in the chorus. We'd released both versions to the public, so it seemed an okay idea.

I did my best for my between-song rants to walk a fine line between humor and respect.

214

"TONIGHT OUR SHOW IS DEDICATED TO THE LATE, GREAT BO SCHEMBECHLER, A MAN SO INSPIRED TO BEAT OHIO STATE THAT HE WILLINGLY GAVE HIS LIFE ON THE EVE OF THE BIGGEST GAME IN THE HISTORY OF THE RIVALRY TO SPUR THE WOVERINES ONTO VICTORY!"

I was kind of shocked that when we sang the O-H-I-O portions of "Buckeye Bop" most of the crowd went ahead with the HEY! HO! FUCK BO! lyrics.

I forget most of what I said that night, but I do remember some of it.

"THAT OLD MAN FUCKED US GOOD ON THE WAY OUT. I THINK HE MAY HAVE DIED ON PURPOSE, JUST TO SPITE US! IF HE'D LIVED ANOTHER FEW HOURS WE'D HAVE BEEN IN THE HILLS WITH THE LOOT. NOW WE'RE GONNA HAVE TO GIVE YOUR HARD-EARNED MONEY TO THE UNIVERSITY OF MICHIGAN!"

And then it was over. People laughed and cried through the whole night. I'll never be sure, but I honestly believe we struck the perfect tone between being funny without being disrespectful of Bo Schembechler. I was as drained as I had ever been before in my life.

I went home the next day and sent a check to Bo's charity that week. A clear picture in my head of a winged bag of money flying away in the direction of Ann Arbor.

Easy come, easy go.

I later heard from his son Schemy via email. He told me that his family had been concerned at what our band was going to do after Bo passed, but that they were very happy with the outcome.

We had planned on retiring the band or at least the band name after that but came back a few years later for a gig. We've played a few times since that fateful night, kicking money to Bo's charity when we turned a profit, but nothing could ever match the sheer insanity of that evening on High Street.

The Ohio State and Michigan game continues to this day, and I hope it will go on long after we're dust. There is something comforting in traditions like it. It gives one a sense of continuity and connection to those who have gone before.

No matter how it pans out, we nailed the name DEAD SCHEMBECHLERS into The Book of The Rivalry, and there's not a fucking thing anyone can do about it.

THE TIME ROBERT PLANT CHARMED THE SHIT OUT OF MY DATE BECAUSE HE'S A ROTTEN LIMEY BASTARD

GETTING LAID WITH A face like mine was never easy. Getting laid with a face like Robert Plant's was always easy. Robert Plant using his face to try to keep my face from getting laid is pretty rotten.

In the fall of 1993, I was again working at WMMR in Philadelphia when Robert Plant, former singer for Led Zeppelin who also boasted a phenomenal solo career, announced two shows at the Tower Theater on his Fate of Nations Tour.

The Tower Theater has always been a favorite place of mine to see rock concerts. Located in Upper Darby, Pennsylvania, just on the outskirts of Philadelphia proper, it first opened in 1929. With a capacity of just over three thousand, its history included a long list of shows I'd witnessed there including Frank Zappa, Jerry Garcia, Peter Gabriel, The Ramones, The Kinks, Utopia, Joan Jett, Thomas Dolby, Ted Nugent, Tears for Fears, Howard Jones, The Pretenders, Squeeze, Eric Idle, Warren Zevon, and many others. It's well regarded by artists and has excellent acoustics.

My future wife and I were dating at this point. She knew little to nothing about rock 'n' roll, so it was fun for me to introduce her to all of the music that I loved, as well as to bring her out to see artists for the first time. Two of our earliest nights out had been concerts at the Tower Theatre. Our first real date was to see Heart. I later took her back for The Ramones. She became a big fan of theirs because, as she said, "Their concert's not too long and they play all of their hits!" She was also impressed that Johnny Ramone knew everything there was to know about baseball. On another occasion we sat second row center for Bob Dylan, where she promptly fell asleep from boredom. I woke her up with a dig of my elbow at one point, saying, "Bob Dylan is giving you the stink eye! Wake the fuck up!"

When Robert Plant's shows came to the theatre in November of '93, I had high hopes for the evening. His latest album was excellent, his touring band was supposed to be outstanding, and the set list had a decent chance of a couple of oldies from Led Zeppelin.

Prior to the concert, I'd obtained word that along with my tickets I'd also get a pair of preshow passes for a meet and greet with Robert. As I'd never met anyone from Led Zeppelin up to that point, I was pretty stoked. I told my girlfriend and she smiled, though it didn't seem she was all that excited.

On the night of the show, I picked up my tickets and passes at the will-call window. There was a small handwritten note in the envelope saying to go to the house-left stage entrance in the theatre. When we got there, I couldn't believe my eyes. The line to go backstage looked to be about a hundred people long. The woman at the very front of it was holding a stack of vinyl album covers nearly as tall as she was. Seriously, I think she had every release Plant had ever sung on.

It was then I heard a voice call my name. It was Frankie Sciarra of Atlantic Records, the same gent who figured into my Stevie Nicks story. It was Frankie's job that night to act as liaison between Robert Plant's tour personnel and the rest of the world.

Sciarra spoke into my ear with an annoyed whisper as he gestured to the long line of people waiting to go backstage. "I don't know who the fuck these people are, but I can tell ya they sure as fuck ain't going backstage!" He then grabbed a couple other people and their guests and walked us through the backstage door.

As the Tower is one of these great old theatres, the backstage is like walking into a time machine. Lots of ropes, curtains, and little cubbie holes. Frankie led us halfway into a short hallway and said, "Robert will be out in a few minutes. You can each get one autograph and one picture, then out you go!" I checked my watch and saw we were just a few minutes away from showtime.

That's when he walked up to us. Robert Plant. He looked like some Viking god of rock 'n' roll from a distant, misty past. You could almost hear the soaring vocals from Led Zep's "Immigrant Song" as he came nearer. It seemed his long, golden locks blew back in the breeze, which was strange as we were indoors and there was no wind of any kind.

I reached out to shake his hand and introduced myself, "Hello, Robert. I'm honored to meet you. My name is..."

I was interrupted by Robert, who swept me aside with the hand that I'd reached out to shake so he could get up close to my date.

"Hello, my name is Robert. It's enchanting to meet you," he mewed.

My girlfriend blushed. "I'm Geri. It's nice to meet you, too."

"What do you do, Geri?" asked the lecherous bastard.

"I'm an attorney," she answered.

"Oh, my goodness. Brains and beauty," he said as I fought back the urge to vomit.

As it didn't look like I'd get a word in edgewise, I simply held out the limited-edition copy of Led Zeppelin IV I'd brought with me along with a black Sharpie. Plant didn't even look at it as he scrawled his name across the top, all while making purring sounds at my date.

Frankie then motioned for us to get together for a picture. As Geri was shorter than both Robert and I, we had her stand in the middle. As we lined up for the picture, Plant reached his left arm around Geri's shoulder then casually used his hand to shove me about a foot away from the two of them.

"Click," said the camera shutter.

"Why, you limey fuck," I thought as we were whisked away, Geri waving goodbye to Robert, staring at him with half-lidded eyes of love, though he was already moving onto the next target in his charm offensive.

A few moments later, we were walking back out to the theatre where the long line of people who'd been waiting had apparently just been told they weren't going backstage. The girl with the stack of albums had tears welling up in her eyes.

Geri stopped us right in front of the woman, oblivious to the unhappy scene around her, and still in the thrall of golden-haired rock Adonis, asked in a too loud voice, "So that guy we just met, he's in the Rolling Stones?"

I told you she didn't know much about music.

The short woman dropped her albums and let out a strangled cry as she stared daggers into my date. I pulled at Geri's hand, hissing, "We've gotta go...NOW!"

Then the lights went down, we found our seats, and I watched the entire show hoping Robert Plant would fall and break his fucking ankle.

THE TIME I THOUGHT MY WIFE WAS GONNA KILL ME OVER A FIVE FINGER DEATH PUNCH RING

I HAVE A PRETTY long history with Ivan Moody, the lead singer of Five Finger Death Punch. Our adventures together go back to his time with his previous band, Motograter. For some reason, we hit it off pretty well and Motograter became the very first group to invite me to travel with them on the road.

The situation didn't work out for Ivan with Motograter, and he saw some tough times after he left the band. However, I believed in him and stayed in touch, always reminding him he was a great front man and encouraging him to find another group. For a while, he was working on a musical project with a coworker of mine at XM named John Stevens, but then he took a break for an audition with another band. That band turned out to be Five Finger Death Punch.

Things immediately took off for Five Finger Death Punch (aka FFDP), much to the chagrin of John Stevens. I flew off to see some of their earliest gigs and offer whatever support I could, in addition to touting the band on the air.

When the band later released their *American Capitalist* album in 2011, they invited me to host the tour presser on Sunset Strip in Hollywood. After the event, they pulled me aside and gave me a gold-plated *American Capitalist* ring. It featured the album logo on the front and lions on the side. They were selling steel versions of the ring on their website but made up a few of the gold-plated rings for longtime supporters. I was really touched by the gesture.

I spoke to bandleader Zoltan Bathory about the rings and how they tied into the concept behind the *American Capitalist* album. His answer was quite telling and also gave me a good laugh. He explained how he'd grown up in Eastern Europe and wanted to get to America to have a shot at making his dreams come true. That's why he doesn't understand Americans who are ashamed of making money, because he came here to have fun and make his fortune. It's also why he designed the over-the-top logo for the rings to look like a championship belt. He wanted it to be larger than life.

A few months later, I was backstage with the band in their hometown of Las Vegas, and I noticed Zoltan was wearing an *American Capitalist* ring, but it wasn't gold-plated.

It was solid fucking gold.

And it looked NICE.

I blurted out how amazing the ring was and asked Zoltan if I could examine it more closely. He handed the ring to me and I almost dropped it from the weight. On further examination, I saw that two golden letters on the inside formed his initials "ZB." I'm not much into bling, but this was a great piece of jewelry. I had to have one.

I sheepishly asked, "Hey, Z. If I were to pay for it, would I be able to get one of these made?" He answered, "Of course!

The guy who created it is Rick the Jeweler, he's based in Chicago. I'll give you his contact info. Hit him up, tell him I said you were okay to have one made, and you can work it out with him."

The following week I called Rick the Jeweler. He seemed like a good guy and we ended up shooting the breeze on the phone for half an hour. We knew a lot of the same people and he was delighted Zoltan had given me the go-ahead to get a ring made. However, in all the friendly banter, I forgot to ask just how much the ring would cost. It wasn't until the end of the call that I thought to ask and by then I was already committed.

When he told me the price I almost shit a Krugerrand, but by then I was already committed and couldn't have backed out without looking like a complete ninny. Rick told me the ring would take a month or two to complete.

Within a couple days, I got really busy like I often to do and completely forgot about the ring. Then a few Saturdays later my wife and I were up early. We both were drinking coffee and she sat at the kitchen island opening mail and bills while I checked my phone for any late-night emails.

It was then I heard her voice rising to roar behind me...

"WHO THE FUCK ARE YOU BUYING JEWELERY FOR IN CHICAGO?!?!?"

My groggy brain couldn't comprehend the question, though she didn't give me long to answer.

"WHO THE FUCK ARE YOU BUYING JEWELERY FOR IN CHICAGO?!?!?"

Then I realized. The ring. It must have been the bill from Rick the Jeweler.

I quickly babbled, "IWASN'TBUYINGJEWLERYFOR
ANYBODYWELLACTUALLYIWASBUTIT'SFOR-
MENOTSOMEBODYELSEIT'SAFIVEFINGERDEATH-
PUNCHAMERICAN CAPITALISTRINGANDIWOULD-
NEVERBUYJEWELRYFORANYBODYELSE." My fast thinking answer may have saved my life. I made sure Geri's hands didn't have any kitchen knives and was glad to see her settle back to open the rest of the mail. Then she leapt back up to her feet.

"HOW COULD YOU SPEND THOUSANDS OF DOLLARS ON A FUCKING FIVE FINGER DEATH PUNCH RING?!?!?!"

To that, I didn't have a quick answer. I still don't.

I have the ring on my hand as I type this and wear it most every day. To my knowledge, there were three of them made. Zoltan's, mine, and a third that Zoltan had made for Ivan Moody. I always kid about them as The Three Elven Rings of Heavy Metal. Sadly, Ivan no longer has his. Apparently, Zoltan gave it as gift to Ivan before a big festival show. Ivan, who had a pretty tough childhood without much in the way of material comforts, was really touched by his generosity. He gave Zoltan a hug and they headed out to play for the enormous crowd. When they reached the stage, Ivan threw his arms in the crowd, saying, "It's great to be here!"

The ring flew off his finger into the mosh pit, never to be seen again.

I'm sure someone found the ring. I just can't understand how they could keep it. Why would they not do the right thing with something so personal? Plus, knowing the Five Finger Death Punch guys and how generous they are, if someone had turned the ring in the band would have treated them like a king. I wouldn't have been surprised to see the person showered with gifts from the group along with a ring of their own. Plus, they'd likely have been given a lifetime backstage pass.

If you're reading this and you have Ivan's ring, it's not too late to do the right thing.

THE TIME I WAS BACKSTAGE AND IT WAS EXACTLY LIKE WHAT PEOPLE THINK BACKSTAGE IS LIKE BUT USUALLY NEVER IS

THE IMAGE OF BACKSTAGE at a concert being an endless party filled with sex, drugs, and debaucheries the likes of which have not been seen since the downfall of Rome is the greatest lie in history.

Having attended thousands of concerts and been given access to the whole shebang much of the time, I can authoritatively tell you that there usually ain't shit going on. On an arena tour, there are a bunch of cement-walled rooms containing various offices, a few Spartan dressing rooms, and catering that will open your bowels like Moses parting the Red Sea.

Oh, sure. Back in the day there was apparently plenty of sex and drugs. Backstage was awash in naked bodies glistening with sweat and cocaine flakes. Nubile groupies sucked like an army of Hoover vacuums on a willing carpet of rock stars and roadies. The music world was a vast ocean of decadence with everyone sworn to fun and loyal to none. Or so I'm told.

Then a lot of people OD'd. Others got mutant strains of venereal diseases, which made their weenies look like the face of the guy at the leper colony in *Papillon*. While some forged ahead and took the risks, most decided their penises didn't need to have the appearance of an overripe raspberry, so they either stood down from Fuckon One or began to protect their pricks in prophylactic portioning so elaborate their crotches resembled Christo's *The Wall*.

That's why I sometimes think of guys like Keith Richards, Steven Tyler, or Ozzy as musical Marvel superheroes, or perhaps some kind of rock demigods. They just can't be regular human beings and have lived through all the shit they did, 'cause not everyone can. For every Iggy Pop there are plenty of Keith Moons, Layne Staleys, and John Bonhams, or others who died well before they got to the success they would have/should have attained.

So there were no delusions in my mind of a rock 'n' roll party train as I rolled into the parking lot of the Blockbuster Sony Entertainment Center in Camden, New Jersey, on Saturday morning, July 22, 2000, for the Ozzfest Tour.

I never missed an Ozzfest Tour and they were all solid, but this year was one of the best. The main stage for this stop would feature Ozzy, Pantera, Godsmack, Static-X, Incubus, Methods of Mayhem, and Queens of the Stone Age. The second stage would be coheadlined by Soulfly and Kittie, while also featuring Disturbed, who were still up-and-comers, among others.

It was a usual day for me at one of these things. I got to see little to no music performed as I ran from tour bus to dressing room to tour bus to dressing room, non-stop from late morning to early evening. Of course, I came away with a ton of material for my radio show, so you needn't shed a tear. After I wrapped the last interview, I collapsed at one of the picnic tables the venue had outside catering and sipped water. I never drink alcohol on the job, as it's bad for business. I don't knock other people who do it, but as I've said before, you're there to work, not join the band. Besides, I do and say enough stupid shit when I'm sober; I don't need Jack Daniels assisting me with that.

When Ozzy began his set, I was too late to grab a spot on the side of the stage, so I was going to walk out into the house and watch from there. However, I got sidetracked. Yeah, I know. You're thinking, "How the fuck could you get sidetracked from seeing Ozzy up close for free?"

I'll tell you.

On the way out, I happened to walk past Pantera's dressing room. As I did, the door opened and I saw what some would describe as the ultimate rock 'n' roll heaven, while others would bless themselves, wrap a rosary around their neck, and pray for deliverance from the foul musical demons that had risen up from the heavy metal underworld to wreak a hellish havoc upon the banks of the Delaware River.

The smallish dressing room was crammed with people. There was barely room to move. Band members from many of the groups on the bill that day, along with crew, roadies, and other guests unknown, staggered around with all of the coordination and surety of newborn giraffes. Their red eyes, many no more than slits, stared glassily with pupils as big as dinosaur eggs. Smoke, both tobacco and skanky skunkweed, billowed from inside. The tumult of music, shouting, and singing from inside the cinder-block-walled den of iniquity rivaled the diabolic dissonance from Ozzy onstage. It was foul. It was evil. It was everything my parents had warned me about.

Naturally, I walked right in.

Well, "walked" probably isn't the right word. "Slid" or "elbowed" are words that are likely more on the mark. I made it a few feet into the room then pressed myself up against the wall to try and get out of the way as most of the Ten Commandments were simultaneously broken right before my unbelieving eyes.

I found myself next to Wayne Static of Static-X who, like me, seemed incredulous at the scene that the guys from Pantera had brought down upon the world. Without taking his eyes off the celebration of sin before us, he leaned over to me.

"This is exactly what people think backstage is like..."

"But never is," I finished. "Have you seen it quite like this before?"

"Never," he answered.

I was sober and Wayne appeared to only have a beer in his hand. Everyone else was out of his or her fucking mind. Sully Erna of Godsmack came up to be with a bottle in his hand and grabbed me by the side of the neck.

"Brutus! How the fuck are ya?"

"I'm good, Sully."

"Have a drink," he said, and brought the bottle toward my mouth.

"Nah, I'm good, brother. I gotta drive."

He good-naturedly ribbed me in his thick Boston accent. "Oh, okay. You fucking pussy! Go drive yourself back to pussy town!"

Then he laughed in my face and shouldered his way back into the throng as I continued to survey the commingled mixture of misdeeds. The door to the dressing room's small bathroom opened across from me. There was a small group of guys and girls inside it hunched over the toilet, on which was draped a woman whose pants were pulled down. I assume this was done to make it easier for the lines of cocaine to be laid out on her posterior. The partiers happily Electro-Luxed up the snowbanks of powder as the door slammed back shut.

I thought, "Slamming the door shut was probably a bad idea as it could cause a rush of air that would blow the blow all over the bathroom." I try to be practical, even under difficult conditions.

Over in the corner, the wall of humanity parted for a moment and I caught a glimpse of a tattoo needle being wielded on someone's shoulder. I'm no expert on inking, but I'm pretty sure that our current surroundings were not likely to meet the sanitary standards of most reputable tattoo parlors. The needle flicked skin and brought forth blood though I couldn't hear it sing its song above the din. One of the crew guys stood up for a second on the arm of a chair stretching up with a camera to get an overhead view of the inking before falling backward against the wall. The crowd then again covered my view.

Suddenly, Dimebag Darrell himself was right in front of me. Nose to nose. A wicked grin spread across his face, his breath an omnium-gatherum of booze, weed, and burning amplifier tubes. He called to me above the commotion.

"Having fun, Lou?"

"Of course!"

"You don't look like it. You look like you seen a ghost. Not your scene?"

I laughed nervously and replied, "Honestly, no."

"That's cool, brother. Be yourself." He laughed, "You'll probably outlive us all!"

Then Dime squeezed my shoulder for a moment before fading back into crowd.

What would you have done in the same situation? Would you have grabbed one of Dimebag's patented Black Tooth Grin shots, a lit joint, and started doing lines off some girl's buns? Or would you do what I did?

I left.

Perhaps I was a fucking pussy that day, but getting blotto after what had been a really productive day of interviews had no allure for me, especially considering the multi-hour drive I had coming up. Fun is fun, but picking your teeth out of a telephone pole is not. Besides, as had been the case through much of my life in general and my career specifically, I kinda tend to go my own way. It's probably made me seem like a dick sometimes and likely not helped ingratiate me to the powers that be, but it helps me keep my life on a more even keel. Plus, I think it's a little bit funny at times to be the only sober, non-tattooed, non-pierced fish in the dark sea of rock 'n' roll outlaws.

An outsider amongst outsiders.

I'm okay with that.

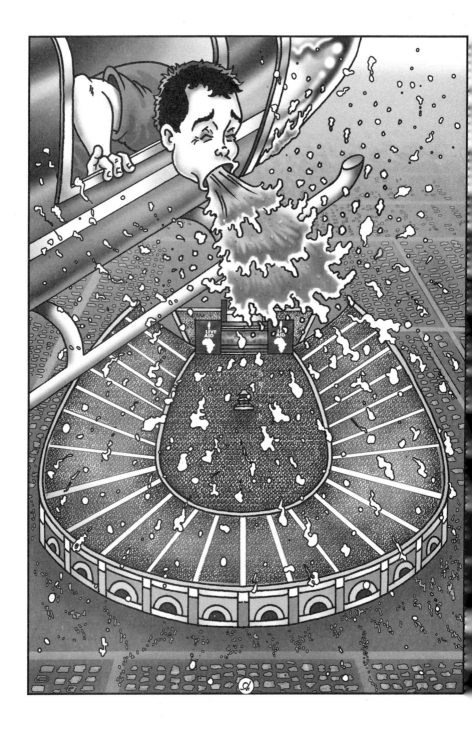

THE TIME I RAINED VOMIT DOWN UPON
THE BIGGEST CONCERT IN HISTORY

MY LIFE HAS BEEN filled with moments of inopportune vomiting. In fact, some of my earliest childhood memories revolve around barfing. My maternal grandmother, known as "Ba" by our family and who lived to the ripe old age of one hundred, was the host for Thanksgiving each year where my family eagerly awaited the post-meal football game in the yard, which inevitably ended with me regurgitating my holiday meal.

"I tackled him and he turned green," said cousin Chris.

"Looks like he's getting ready," opined Uncle John.

Cousin Tommy called to the house, "HERE IT IS, EVERY-BODY. C'MON AND WATCH!"

The family rushed out to the yard abuzz with excitement.

"BRRRRRAAAAAAAAAAAAP," said I.

"Ewwww, the dogs are eating it!"

Such were the family Pilgrim fests growing up in English-town, New Jersey.

However, as seen elsewhere in this tome you're currently reading, vomiting at key moments is not unusual for me. Even at the biggest concert event in history: Live Aid. Live Aid was the massive, dual-continent benefit show held on Saturday, July 13, 1985. Conceptualized by rocker Bob Geldof to raise money for hunger relief during the Ethiopian famine, it was held at both Wembley Stadium in London and John F. Kennedy Stadium in Philadelphia. Start times were staggered with London beginning at 7:00 a.m. EDT then Philly kicking in at 9:00 a.m. During the portion of the day when both concerts were happening, the two cities alternated between their acts as the other crowd watched on giant video screens in their respective stadium. It was carried on television and radio around the world, giving birth to the modern benefit show concept before wrapping up at 11:05 p.m. Eastern Time that night.

I threw up on the crowd in Philadelphia. All 100,000 of them. Allow me to explain.

The summer of Live Aid, I was into my second year at WMMR in Philadelphia working as morning show producer and weekend DJ. We were thrilled when the show was announced, as it would be just a few miles from our studios in Center City. Local promoter Electric Factory Concerts would oversee the American half of the event, though legendary concert impresario Bill Graham would be on hand to guide the stage production. Our radio staff was less than excited when we learned we wouldn't carry the actual music as the contract to do so was given to the affiliated network of the competing radio station in town, WYSP. However, instead of giving up, WMMR teamed up with our sister station WNEW-FM/New York. Though we couldn't legally carry the music, we planned on trying to storm the backstage press areas by pooling our staffs, setting up a broadcast truck behind the stage, and providing listeners in Philly, New York, and other markets around the country with exclusive interviews and coverage.

The fact that we were contractually forbidden from actually being there was just a small kink we'd work out that day.

The full lineup was like something out of a classic rock radio dream. London boasted Paul McCartney, Elton John, The Who, David Bowie, U2, Sting with Phil Collins, and many other performances, including what many would consider the greatest of all time: the set from Queen, which was later immortalized in the film *Bohemian Rhapsody*. The lineup for us in Philly was nothing to sneeze at either, as it included Bob Dylan, Black Sabbath, Eric Clapton, The Cars, Tom Petty and the Heartbreakers, Madonna, Santana, The Beach Boys, Judas Priest, and local stars The Hooters, among many others. Our show would also feature short reunions by both Crosby, Stills, Nash & Young and Led Zeppelin. Filling in for the late John Bonham on drums would be Phil Collins, who planned on performing in London then flying on the supersonic Concorde jet from London to New York City before heading to the stadium for our show. It looked like it was gonna be a pretty good day of music.

About a week out from the show, one of the local crew guys I knew pulled me aside at my regular watering hole, J. C. Dobbs on South Street. He told me he'd been contracted to do the monitor mix for Duran Duran during their rehearsal the day before the concert. He gave me the address of the studio on Front Street along with the time they were scheduled to arrive. He couldn't give me permission to watch, but I could wait in the lobby and try to talk my way into an interview.

The band arrived early that Friday afternoon. The limo pulled up to the front and the first people out of it were two extremely scary bodyguards. Seeing me in the lobby, they ran right at me and began to yell at me in cockney accents. "WHO THE FUCK ARE YOU? YOU'RE NOT SUPPOSED TO BE HERE! CLEAR OUT, MATE! DO IT NOW!"

I could only hold up my arms in a pitiful effort to ward off the blows I expected to rain down on me, but when I lowered them, another far calmer Englishman stood before me.

"Who are you and why are you here?" he asked.

"I'm from WMMR and I heard the band was going to be here, and I'll sit quietly and not make a sound and if any of the guys have even a few moments I'd love to get a few questions in with them and then I'll get out of your hair forever, it would really mean a lot and I'd very much appreciate it but either way please don't let those other two guys kill me 'cause I'm too young to die."

The Englishman laughed at me, saying, "All right, then. Sit in the corner and I'll send someone your way when they have time." The two guards came over and slapped my back, saying, "Sorry, mate. Just doing our jobs. No hard feelings." If I remember correctly, they had both previously been Royal Marines. I thanked them for not murdering me.

At this point in time, Duran Duran was one of the biggest bands in the world. They'd started in what would later be known as alternative, crossed over to pop, but remained rock enough in their style for stations like WMMR to play. They certainly didn't act like big rock stars and seemed quite friendly, coming over to chat with me during their breaks, with the official interview being done by singer Simon Le Bon. They ran through all four songs they'd perform at the concert including "Union of the Snake," "Save A Prayer," "The Reflex," and "A View to a Kill." The last title was their recent James Bond theme song and led to the best part of the rehearsal. As they'd never performed it live before, no one in the group could remember how it went, so they were going back and forth to the control room, where the engineer had a cassette of the tune. They each cocked their ears trying to figure out the notes and chords. I thought they were pretty chill about the whole thing, considering they'd have to perform the following day with half the fucking planet watching. As I had to get up before dawn, I left in the middle of the evening. Later in 2007, I hosted an XM Satellite Radio Artist Confidential with them and we had a good laugh about our previous time together.

Finally, it was show day. As I was the junior member of the air staff, I would begin the early morning on the air in the studio. However, I would get to head to the stadium later in the morning to join in with the coverage. Then, a couple of days before the show, I was called into the office of our program director Ted Utz, who had a question.

"Have you ever ridden in a helicopter?

"Uhhhh, no."

"Then I have good news for you!"

The plan was for me to get off the air, head to the heliport at the end of Spring Garden Street in Philadelphia along the Delaware River, and then fly over the stadium with a two-way radio to give eye-in-the-sky reports.

Visions of the wrecked chopper in the film version of M*A*S*H began to dance through my head.

When the morning of the show arrived, I began my day according to plan with my in-studio air shift. Every artist I played was someone who would be part of the festivities for the show and each of my breaks was taken up with information for the concertgoers, including a list of what you could bring in, as well as warnings regarding the weather, which was expected to be hot and humid.

My shift in the studio ended; I rushed down to the corner of Nineteenth and Walnut streets across from Rittenhouse Square, hailed a green Quaker City Cab with one hand as I held the two-way radio in the other, then headed to the heliport.

I arrived to find the copter waiting and ready to go. The pilot told me he considered this a "milk run." In other words, a super-easy flight with no turbulence and a very smooth ride. My confidence in the whole endeavor began to rise as I climbed onboard, strapped myself into the copilot position, and we rose straight up.

Let's return for a moment to my personal vomiting history, shall we? Along with the unfortunate-but-regular Thanksgiving gagging, I could always be counted on to turn any carnival ride into a vomit comet. Well, not exactly. I've always been fine on roller coasters regardless of how high or fast they go. However, put me on a child's teacup ride and I turn into a stomach-acid-spewing version of a lawn sprinkler. As long as I'm moving in a straight line, it's all good, man. However, if you put me on anything with a circular motion, you'll soon know what my previous meal was made up of.

Which brings us back to the helicopter. As we rose straight up then moved straight forward toward the Ben Franklin Bridge, which linked downtown Philadelphia with

Camden, New Jersey, across the river, I felt like I was in a scene from *Apocalypse Now*. I sang the melody to "Ride of the Valkyries" into my radio to test the signal.

"DA NA NA NA NA NA, DA NA NA NA NA NA!"

Then the pilot banked heavily to the right and I looked straight down into the river out of my side door.

"DA NA NA NA NA NAAAAAAAAAAAAAAAAAAAAAAA!!! GET ME OUTTA HERE!!!"

My pilot laughed, the sound mocking me in the headset, and brought the copter higher. And higher. And higher. We got pretty fucking high. I hadn't been that high since my days of sucking balloons filled with nitrous oxide in the parking lots of Grateful Dead concerts. Not only did we bank from side to side, which caused the bile to rise to the back of my throat, but I was also disconcerted by the view between my feet as the helicopter's nose was made of glass. My skin felt cool and clammy though beads of sweat formed on my forehead and my butt crack felt like one of the of the Jersey swamps of home.

Finally, we reached our steady altitude as we neared the Walt Whitman Bridge with JFK Stadium waiting just beyond. The staff back in the radio studio barked at me over the two-way and I sent back a couple of reports containing weather and traffic conditions along with observations about the crowd below. By now, my stomach had settled and I was feeling pretty good again about the flight. It was then my pilot suggested we "circle" around the area.

I wish he hadn't.

As he banked the copter, I felt the rush rising up from my belly. Leaning forward, I placed my head between my knees, and as I stared down through the glass at the greatest humanitarian gesture ever taken up by music artists in the history of mankind, I puked all over the floor.

"WHAT THE FUCK ARE YOU DOING?" cried the less-than-pleased pilot as the stink rose from the plexiglass.

I then reached up to the tiny sliding window, which made up a small portion of the door on my side of the copter. I slid it open, stuck my mouth through, and sent a deluge of gastrointestinal expectoration out into the air where it was sucked up by the rotor blades and distributed over the crowd far below. While still only late morning, the heat and humidity were already suffocating the concert attendees, and I like to believe that my rotor-bladed belly brew eventually fell as welcome droplets of cooling moisture on the faces of those who most needed respite from the sweltering conditions on that landmark day.

We soon after landed at the heliport where the pilot gave me a "relief bag" before our second flight. It was far less eventful, and after we returned from the second flight, I hailed a cab to take me down to the stadium.

It had already been an eventful morning for the combined WMMR and WNEW staff members at the show. Unable to get backstage passes at first, the day seemed lost. It was then that New York radio legend Scott Muni of WNEW, one of the DJs I grew up worshipping, flagged down promoter Bill Graham. The program director for WNEW at the time was Charlie Kendall, who a few years earlier held the same job at WMMR where he hired me as an intern, giving me my start in the business. Charlie explained years later, "No one was allowed in until Bill Graham saw Muni from about fifty yards away. He smiled, waved his hand, and we had full access."

This allowed us to roam everywhere backstage with the exception of the artist lounge and dressing rooms. However, we could get to the press areas and catering to begin grabbing the musicians for interviews. Things were already cooking along when I arrived from the helicopter, washed the dried puke off my chin, hung the white "PRESS AID" laminated pass around my neck, and began to work.

Quick aside, I still have that pass as well as another laminate from the show. Given to me shortly after the concert from my friend "JR" who worked for Electric Factory Concerts, the other is a "Performer Z" stage pass, which he told me was Tom Petty's. As JR had a ton of other passes from the show, he kindly gave me that one.

The first artist I was able to wrangle was Carlos Santana. He was preparing for his five-song set, which would also feature jazz guitarist Pat Metheny. Carlos was absolutely buzzing from the positive vibe of the day. Interviewing big artists was still something new to me. I'd done a few, but nothing ever under such high-pressure conditions. However, Carlos couldn't have been nicer and enjoyed the questions enough to invite me to be his guest when he played Philly again a couple of weeks later at the Mann Music Center. Philly radio DJ Cyndy Drue snapped a shot of me walking by with Carlos which is one of only two photos I have from the day, the other being with my old friend, Pierre Robert of WMMR.

I watched the entire music world flashing by me. As most of the backstage crewmembers worked for the local promotion company Electric Factory Concerts, and many of them were my drinking buddies, I found as the day went on that I got more and more access even as the areas allowed to the press began to shrink.

As is the case at these events, I saw very little of the music that day. I did make it a point to catch a bit of Crosby, Stills, Nash & Young, who at first didn't seem like they'd perform until Bill Graham convinced them to do so. Graham was amazing that day and always willing to get his hands dirty for the cause. At one point I watched him throw his clipboard down in disgust when the rotating drum platform got stuck until he managed to shove it forward while down on his hands and knees, cursing like a sailor the whole time. I saw Phil Collins when he arrived backstage, looking unshaven and pale following his set at the London venue, the transatlantic flight, and then the shuttle to Philly. Phil's solo set for the JFK Stadium crowd was the same two songs he'd sung lead on with Sting in London, "Against All Odds" and "In the Air Tonight." He sounded good, though he seemed a bit dazed. However, the short set he performed with Led Zeppelin was, to be honest, kind of disappointing. Robert Plant's voice was weak, Jimmy Page's guitar was out of tune, and John Paul Jones had a look on his face like he knew they were sinking. The drumming by Phil Collins and Tony Thompson did its best, but it all fell flat. There was a night and day difference between this Live Aid performance and their triumphant reunion at London's O2 Arena, which I attended in 2007.

At some point that afternoon, I went back to the enormous camper the radio stations had set up just outside the backstage entrance, which acted as our nerve center. It was from there that we were uplinking the audio to the radio stations around the country. While crude by today's standards, it was an ingenious method to cover the concerts, and our ground coverage was better than anything the official network was offering. As I walked into the weak but welcome air conditioning in the vehicle, I saw Scott Muni, his face purple from the heat. Scott had been doing radio since the early 1960s and helped invent FM Rock radio. Though he was a legend making a comfortable living on WNEW, and as a voice-over talent for things like *Monday Night Football*, he was out there in the sweltering humidity busting his ass like the rest of us. As a guy who was on a first-name basis with all of the Beatles and all of the Rolling Stones, he sent a good example with his work ethic.

Scott could also drink *anyone* under the table.

That thought, however, was far from my mind when I walked in and saw him. I was just overcome with elation to be in the same zip code as one of the people responsible for me wanting to be on the radio in the first place. I walked up to Scott to introduce myself, and as I was parched from the heat, asked if I could have a hit of the apple juice he was drinking. He stopped me immediately in his deeper than the Mines of Moria growl.

"Hold on, kid! That's the real hooch!"

I held up the glass and sniffed. It was Johnny Walker Black.

Heat, humidity, and all, Scott was drinking straight scotch. Even Keith Richards's liver would have whimpered at the thought.

Wishing to impress him, I held up the glass and asked, "May I?"

His face immediately brightened. "Help yourself, kid!"

I downed a slug of the wretched brown liquid and felt it burn the back of my throat, already seared from the stomach acid churned up during my helicopter rides. This was enough to impress Muni. He called over Utz and Kendall who were running the broadcast.

"Fats here is with me now."

This statement was important on two levels. One, it meant he had noticed I knew the local crew guys and was able to get venue access, which made me valuable. Two, he called me "Fats." Now Scott was never good at names, but if he liked you, he'd call you "Fats." Being bestowed with the moniker "Fats" by Scott Muni was the radio equivalent of receiving the Presidential Medal of Freedom. I was glued to him the next several hours and could not believe the ease with which he moved amongst the giants of the music world. Even Keith Richards and Ronnie Wood of The Rolling Stones, who would back Bob Dylan toward the end of the concert, performing a set that included "Blowing in the Wind," hugged Scott when they saw him. I was happy just to swim in this guy's wake.

About the only time I could remember coming to a full stop was around 7:00 p.m. I had popped into catering, actually a special Hard Rock Café that was set up for the event (I still have the menu I stole) to get some water, and noticed that the usual buzzing of voices had died down backstage. It was then that I looked up at the bank of television sets above the table and chairs and there he was.

Freddie Mercury.

Queen was in the middle of their set. The one that would go down in history. The set that would eventually rack up something like 150,000,000 views on YouTube. I owned all of their albums on 8-track growing up, with *A Night at the Opera* and *News of the World* being my faves. Never got to see them though. I had tickets twice but ended up sick both times. As they were a regular touring band, I always thought I'd get another chance to catch them. It never happened. Those few minutes I stood in catering in Philadelphia, watching Queen put to shame every other artist who performed that day, was the closest I ever got to Freddie Mercury, though I was in London years later to cover the Freddie Mercury Tribute show after he passed away. And I didn't even get to see Queen's whole set that day as I had to run off to the next interview. However, for those scant moments it was like being under a spell. I would be tempted to trade all of my other many concert experiences to have been in London for just that one set.

As Live Aid pushed toward its conclusion and darkness fell over South Philadelphia, security had become tighter and far less pleasant. A guard stopped me near the stage and seemed ready to walk me out. Luckily, at that moment one of the crew guys I knew saw my peril and swept in. For the life of me, I can't remember his name, but I recall he worked at J. C. Dobbs and was an excellent skateboarder. He put his arm around my shoulder and said, "Stick your recorder in my face and walk."

So I did.

We held a mock interview as he walked me deeper and deeper into the grounds. He had a high-level pass and took me past countless checkpoints until we stood in the holiest-of-holies: The Artist's Lounge.

He then slapped me on the back and whispered, "You're on your own now."

And then he was gone.

The Artist's Lounge at Live Aid was a series of small trailers in a semi-circle a little ways behind the stage. Over the center was a tented section set up like a sheik's playroom in the desert. There were couches, big pillows, and racks of television monitors.

I soft-shoed further inside as I slipped my PRESS AID pass into my shirt pocket and hid my recorder in my jeans. Both would have been a dead giveaway that I had no fucking business being back there, and if I'd asked anyone for an interview, I'd have immediately been dished. Simon Le Bon from Duran Duran noticed me and gave me a wave hello. I smiled and nodded my head back and looked around the oversized room. It was a who's who of music including Madonna, Neil Young, Phil Collins, Eric Clapton, The Cars, Tom Petty, and who the fuck knows who else. I was right at the center of the rock 'n' roll universe.

And I was completely screwed.

Instead of being elated to be there, I was in mortal terror. If they discovered that I wasn't supposed to be in the private lounge, not only would I be beaten like a ginger stepchild, I'd die of embarrassment at being called out in front of half the major rock stars on the planet, the other half having finished up already in London. Not knowing what to do, I faded to just outside of the tent, on the edge of the light from the televisions, which were then showing Mick Jagger wrapping up "It's Only Rock 'n' Roll (But I Like It)" with Tina Turner, The Temptations, and Hall & Oates. A couple of serious looking bodyguards sauntered into the area, and I thought it was time to go.

But where?

I slowly stepped backward into the dark, then sidled into the small no-man's land in between the lounge and the stage. It was poorly lit there and gave me more of a feeling of safety as I planned my exit strategy. Then from the direction of the stage, some motion caught my eye. Heading right toward me was Mick Jagger.

Was this really happening?

I looked around and there was no one else nearby. No bodyguards. No security. No road crew. No one. Mick was coming at me as he headed back to the dressing room area. I pulled my recorder out of jeans and got ready.

As Mick got closer, he slowed his pace and stopped. His eyes fell to my recorder, and you could see the look on his face change to one of sad resignation. As he looked up at me it was as if his eyes said, "I'll answer your question, but I really don't want you to ask one."

Getting even one minute with Mick Jagger would have been an enormous feather in my cap. I'd have bragging rights better than anyone else covering the show in the United States. I would be showered with praise. Statues would be erected in my honor. Schoolchildren would memorize my birthday in history books. The sun would shine directly out of my ass there in the darkness.

However, I didn't wanna be a jerk.

I said, "If they find out I could have done an interview, they'll sack me for sure. Off you go, Mick."

Jagger smiled and jogged away in the direction of the dressing rooms.

I slunk off into the darkness, navigating around the security until I found my way back to our broadcast trailer. I couldn't realize if not pressing the issue with Mick Jagger was the coolest thing I'd ever done or the stupidest.

Maybe a bit of both.

The night ended with Scott Muni inviting all of us youngsters back to his hotel. We walked through the dark to where my coworker Kevin Gunn had the only car among us. After fumbling around awhile to find the vehicle in the post-concert murk, we finally came to a stop in front of his tiny Dodge Colt. It was a car that would seat two adults comfortably.

There were eight of us.

After a few moments of embarrassed silence, we heard Scott's voice growl to Kevin in the dark, "Well, Fats. I guess we know where *we're* sitting!"

We all laughed then loaded in the car, six of us stacked like firewood in the tiny back seat, Muni and Gunn in the front. When we got to the hotel bar, Scott wouldn't let anyone spend a cent, saying, "You kids earned it."

After a few minutes, he came over and bought me a shot of Jack Daniels. He toasted me with his Johnny Walker.

"Good working with you, Fats."

I just smiled and kept my fucking mouth shut about Mick Jagger.

POSTFACE

MY PARENTS, PAT AND Louie, grew up on the mean streets of Newark, New Jersey, and were filled with wisdom beyond their years. It was when I was a year or two old that we moved to the farmlands outside of Englishtown, New Jersey. Mom started an antiques business that concentrated on books, while Dad worked in construction for Local 825 of the International Union of Operating Engineers.

They would often give me life advice, much of which I was too stupid to follow.

It was sometime in 1984 or 1985, early in my career while first at WMMR in Philadelphia, that I was back home visiting them and whiffed on two of the best pieces of advice I ever got.

Fixing breakfast in the kitchen that morning, Mom said, "You should take better care of your hearing. You go to so many of these loud concerts. Are you protecting your ears?"

"Never!" I laughed. "I love it loud! And if tinnitus is good enough for Pete Townshend of The Who then it's good enough for me!"

Dad just rolled his eyes and let out a cloud of Lucky Strike smoke in my direction.

"Well, if being around music is going to be your livelihood, you'd better protect your hearing," she said.

I didn't. Now I have severe hearing loss and constant ringing in my ears...because I'm an idiot.

Mom continued, "And you're already getting to do interesting things like meeting famous people and traveling to exotic events. One day you'll want to write books about it all. You should start keeping a journal. It doesn't have to detailed, just write a few notes each day about what you did and that will key your memory later."

I laughed again, "I already remember everything. Besides, I don't have time to write stuff down."

I never did start that journal. I sure wish that I had. This book would have been completed years ago and would have been much easier to write. Shit, I'd have ten books by now.

Dad then added something he said to me on many occasions. I think it's an original quote from him, as I've researched it and have never found it anywhere else. I've always thought it quite profound.

Sipping his coffee he opined, "Books are the candles that light men's minds."

I smiled in agreement and asked, "Even rock 'n' roll books?"

He shrugged his shoulders.

"Sure, why not?"

ACKNOWLEDGEMENTS

WRITING A BOOK IS as much fun as you can have with something that is a gigantic pain in the ass. There are many people who have made writing this particular book less painful than it could have been.

Thank you to my literary agent Bob Diforio and D4EO Literary Agency. They're the folks you want to reach out to for the film rights. At the very least, someone should make a movie out of the Dead Schembechlers chapter. Seriously, get it to Cameron Crowe. He'll know what to do. I should also thank Paul Rapp (a.k.a. Lee Harvey Blotto) for putting me in touch with D4EO in the first place, as well as for the opening drum riff on "I Wanna Be A Lifeguard."

The entire staff at Rare Bird Books has been splendid to deal with through the birthing of this thing. I'm relieved that my endless rookie questions didn't drive them insane.

Alan MacBain not only did the illustrations for this book, he has been providing me with wonderful graphic embellishments for decades. I am glad for both his talent and friendship these many years. Plus, Alan has a vast knowledge of *MAD* magazine and rock 'n' roll, which is always admirable in a person.

It was Corey Taylor who helped kick start the book *finally* getting finished. He came to me about a year ago with the foreword ready to go, asking why I wasn't done yet. I hemmed and hawed that I still had chapters to add. He looked at me as if I were the stupidest person the planet and said, "You fucking idiot! Just write another book after this one!" I thank him for that and everything else.

There were many people who took time for questions about the publishing world or who eyeballed the material for me. They include Joe Oestreich, Rick O'Brien, Ken Sharp, Martin Goldsmith, and Jennifer Kunkle. Countless others reached out with suggestions of which stories to put in the book.

Big ups to the crew from *hardDrive with Lou Brutus* including Andy Denemark, Nick Verbitsky, Randy Hawke, Paul Spagna, Bill Powell, and Zak Tranese. A special mention goes to Roxy Myzal for the many years she produced the show and constantly yelled at me so I wouldn't be late for my interviews. Further thanks to every radio station, programmer, and DJ who has supported the program. Extra gratitude to the board ops and other folks who have physically gotten the show on the air.

I must also mention the people I've worked with through the years at SiriusXM including Scott Greenstein, Dara Altman, Steve Blatter, and Dave Wellington.

Thank you to Cheap Trick just for being Cheap Trick.

I also wish to express my gratitude to every band, musician, artist, artist manager, tour manager, crew member, technician, roadie, sound engineer, monitor mixer, lighting person, follow spot operator, photographer, videographer, promoter, producer, talent booker, publicist, record company rep, security professional, venue owner, will call window worker, ticket taker, merch seller, concessionaire, travel agent, driver, consultant, accountant, caterer, cook, waiter, waitress, bartender, janitor, fellow media member, and everyone else from every rock show I've ever attended. They are all important to the experience and none of them get enough credit.

I am sincerely sorry to not cite each person who deserves to be singled out here individually. However, as I've joked with him for years that if I wrote a book, I would mention him by name, three cheers and a tiger for Stephen Shaw who **always** made sure I got a full set of tour passes.

A loving thanks to my family including my wife, Geri, my daughter, Jilly, and Darla the Wonder Dog for everything they do to keep me grounded in reality. Oh, Aunt Min and Uncle Gene, too. Hi, Aunt Min! And I will take this opportunity to remind Jilly of what Ed Sheeran once told her backstage, "You've got the coolest fucking Dad ever!" I will never let her hear the end of it. LOL

My final acknowledgment goes to you who have supported in any way this crazy rock 'n' roll shit I've been lucky enough to be a part of. Whether you listen on the radio or go to the shows or buy the T-shirts, without you, there is nothing. That is a fact. I thank you all.

APPENDIX: THE LIST

MY GUESSTIMATE IS THAT I've attended over three thousand music events. This includes mega-festivals down to tiny local shows, which would be hard-pressed to be called a "concert." What follows is an incomplete list of performers I've seen in person with those I've interviewed being **bolded**. I've included a handful of comedians I've seen perform in concert settings, too.

Many of the artists I've seen on numerous occasions with just a few examples being Frank Zappa (10+), Papa Roach (20+), KoRn (25+), KISS (25+), Rob Zombie (25+), Sevendust (30+), Cheap Trick (35+), Disturbed (40+), Slipknot (40+), The Ramones (50), and the Grateful Dead (including related side projects, 125+).

After this is published, I will no doubt find missing acts that should have been included. For example, when giving this appendix a final look I noticed Dead & Company, a group I've seen numerous times and have worked with as Program Director for SiriusXM's Grateful Dead Channel, wasn't listed. Once this is set to page, I shall be driven insane by what I missed.

Please note that I've kept every bit of memorabilia from these shows including the tickets, passes, posters, guitar picks, set lists, and various band gear. Many of the items are covered in signatures. Maybe one day they'll make a nifty book on their own.

10 YEARS
12 STONES
14-KARAT GOLD
2CENTS
311
38 SPECIAL
3 DOORS DOWN
3 PILL MORNING
40 BELOW SUMMER
4TH FLOOR
5 SECONDS OF SUMMER
6 GIG
7TH CYCLE
805
80's KISS
9TH PLANET OUT, THE
A.D.D.
ABYDOS
AC/DC
ACCEPT
ACILLATEM
ACTION BRONSON
ADAMS, BRYAN
ADAMS, RYAN
A DAY TO REMEMBER
ADELITAS WAY
ADEMA
ADKINS, TRACE
A DOZEN FURIES

AEGES
AEOUS
AEROSMITH
AFI
A FLOCK OF SEAGULLS
AGAINST ME!
AGGROLITES, THE
AIRBOURNE
AIR SUPPLY
ALBERT, HERB
ALICE IN CHAINS
ALIEN ANT FARM
A LIGHT DIVIDED
ALKALINE TRIO
ALLMAN, GREGG
ALLMAN BROTHERS, THE
ALL THAT REMAINS
ALTERBEAST
ALTER BRIDGE
AMEN
AMERICAN BANG
AMERICAN FANGS
AMERICAN HEAD CHARGE
A MIGHTY WIND
AMIGO THE DEVIL
AMITY AFFLICTION, THE
AMON AMARTH
ANBERLIN
ANDERSON, JON

ANDERSON, LAURIE
ANDREW WK
ANEW REVOLUTION
ANGEL
ANGEL DU$T
ANOTHER ANIMAL
ANOTHER LOST YEAR
ANTHEM
ANTHRAX
ANTI FLAG
ANTI MORTEM
ANTISTAR
AOD
APARTMENT TWENTY SIX
A PERFECT CIRCLE
APEX THEORY
APHASIA
APOCALYPTICA
APPLE, FIONA
AQUABATS, THE
ARANDA
ARCH ENEMY
ARCHITECTS
ARENA
ARMOR FOR SLEEP
ARMY OF ANYONE
ART OF DYING
ART OF NOISE, THE
ASHES DIVIDE
ASIA
A-SIDES, THE
AS I LAY DYING
ASKING ALEXANDRIA
AS LIONS
A'S, THE
ATOMSHIP

ATREYU
ATTACK! ATTACK!
AT THE DRIVE IN
ATTIKA 7
ATTILA
AUDIO KARATE
AUDIOSLAVE
AUDIOVENT
AUNT FLOSSIE
AUTHORITY ZERO
AUTISTIC BEHAVIOR
AUTOMATIC BLACK
AUTUMN BURNING
AVATAR
AVENGED SEVENFOLD
AWAKEN THE SHADOW
AZALEA, IGGY
B-52'S, THE
BABYMETAL
BACHMAN TURNER OVERDRIVE
BAD BRAINS
BAD COMPANY
BADFLOWER
BAD RELIGION
BAD REMEDY
BAD SEED RISING
BAD WOLVES
BAEZ, JOAN
BAND, THE
BANGLES, THE
BANNED FROM UTOPIA
BARONESS
BARTON, RACHEL
BASEMENT
BAY, JAMES
BAZZI

BEACH BOYS

BEARTOOTH

BEASTIE BOYS

BEAUTIFUL CREATURES

BECK

BEDOUIN SOUNDCLASH

BEER FOR DOLPHINS

BENETAR, PAT

BENSON, GEORGE

BERU REVUE

BETTY BLOWTORCH

BETWEEN THE BURIED & ME

BEWARE OF DARKNESS

BEYOND THRESHOLD

BIAFRA, JELLO

BIEBER, JUSTIN

BIFFY CLYRO

BIG COUNTRY

BIG MEANIE

BIG SUGAR

BIG WRECK

BILLY FALCON AND BURNING
 ROSE

BIOHAZARD

BLACK, FRANK

BLACK COFFEE

BLACK CROWES, THE

BLACK DAHLIA MURDER, THE

BLACK EYED PEAS

BLACK FIRES, THE

BLACKFOOT

BLACK LABEL SOCIETY

BLACK LIGHT BURNS

BLACK 'N BLUE

BLACK PISTOL FIRE

BLACK RAINBOW

BLACK SABBATH

BLACKSTONE CHERRY

BLACK SUNSHINE

BLACK TIDE

BLACKTOP MOJO

BLACK VEIL BRIDES

BLANK THEORY

BLEEDING BACK

BLEEKER

BLINDSIDE

BLINK 182

BLONDIE

BLOODHOUND GANG

BLOTTO

BLUE MAN GROUP

BLUE ÖYSTER CULT

BLUES BROTHERS, THE

BLUNT, JAMES

BOBAFLEX

BOBBY AND THE MIDNITES

BODY COUNT

BOGART, DEANNA

BOILER ROOM

BONAMASSA, JOE

BONDS, GARY U. S.

BONHAM, JASON

BON JOVI

BOOKER T AND THE MG'S

BOSTON MANOR

BOWIE, DAVID

BOWLING FOR SOUP

BOY SETS FIRE

BRAINS, THE

BRAVERY, THE

BREAKING BENJAMIN

BREAKING POINT

CLAY, ANDREW "DICE"

CLAYPOOL, LES

CLEOPATRICK

CLINTON, GEORGE

CLOCKWORK

CLUTCH

COAL CHAMBER

COCHRANE, TOM

COCKBURN, BRUCE

COCK ROBIN

CODE ORANGE

COHEED AND CAMBRIA

COLD

COLD KINGDOM

COLDPLAY

COLDSPELL

COLLECTIVE SOUL

COLLINS, ALBERT

COLLINS, PHIL

COLLINS, SANDRA

COLOURING LESSON

CONNICK, HARRY, JR.

CONSULT THE BRIEFCASE

CONWELL, TOMMY

COOPER, ALICE

COPELAND, SHEMEKIA

CORNELL, CHRIS

CORNELL, TONI

COSTELLO, ELVIS

COUGAR, JOHN

COUNTING CROWS

COVER YOUR TRACKS

COWBOY MOUTH

CRACKER

CRADLE OF FILTH

CRAGARS, THE

CRASH BOOM BANG

CRASHING ATLAS

CRAVING THEO

CRAY, ROBERT

CRAZY TOWN

CREED

CROBOT

CROOKED X

CROSBY, DAVID

CROSBY, STILLS, NASH &
  YOUNG

CROSBY, STILLS & NASH

CROSBY & NASH

CROSSBREED

CROSSFADE

CROW, SHERYL

CROWN JEWELS, THE

CROWN THE EMPIRE

CRUZADOS

CRY WOLF

CULT, THE

CULTURE CLUB

CURRY, TIM

CUTE LEPERS

CYPRESS HILL

CYRUS, BILLY RAY

CYRUS, MILEY

DALE, DICK

DAMAGE PLAN

DAMNED THINGS, THE

DAMNWELLS, THE

DAMN YANKEES

DAMONE

DANCE GAVIN DANCE

DANKO JONES

DANZIG

DARKEST HOUR

DARKNESS, THE

DARK NEW DAY

DARWIN'S THEORY

DASH RIP ROCK

DAVE MATTHEWS BAND

DAVIES, DAVE

DAVIES, RAY

DAVIS, SPENCER

DEAD & COMPANY

DEAD KENNEDYS

DEADLIGHTS

DEAD PETS

DEAD SCHEMBECHLERS

DEADSET SOCIETY

DEADSY

DEAFHEAVEN

DEAF PEDESTRIANS

DEATH FROM ABOVE 1979

DECYFER DOWN

DED

DEEP PURPLE

DEF LEPPARD

DEFTONES

DELLACOMA

DEMOB HAPPY

DEPSWA

DERULO, JASON

DESTINY'S CHILD

DETECTIVE

DEUCE

DEVICE

DEVILDRIVER

DEVIL TO DRAG

DEVIL WEARS PRADA, THE

DEVO

DIAMANTE

DICKIES, THE

DIDDLEY, BO

DIECAST

DILLINGER ESCAPE PLAN

DI MEOLA, AL

DIMMU BORGIR

DINOSAUR PILE-UP

DIR EN GREY

DIRE STRAITS

DIRTY HONEY

DIRTY LITTLE RABBITS

DISHWALLA

DISTILLERS, THE

DISTURBED

DIVINYLS, THE

DIVYDED

DJ RAP

DJ Z TRIP

DOGFIGHT

DOKKEN

DOLBY, THOMAS

DOMMIN

DON BROCO

DOOBIE BROTHERS

DOPE

DOROTHY

DOWN

DOWNPLAY

DOWNSET

DOWN THE SUN

DR. JOHN

DR. NEPTUNE

DRAGON FORCE

DRAG PIPE

DRAIN STH

DREAD ZEPPELIN
DREAMING, THE
DREAM THEATRE
DRESDEN DOLLS, THE
DRIVE A
DRIVIN N CRYIN
DROGE, PETE
DROID
DROP BOX
DROPKICK MURPHYS
DROPKICK WOODYS
DROWNING POOL
DUCK TAPE
DUCKY BOYS
DUPREE, NIGEL
DURAN DURAN
DURBIN, JAMES
DUST N' BONES
DUST TO DUST
DYLAN, BOB
EAGLES, THE
EARLY PEARL
EARSHOT
ECHO AND THE BUNNYMEN
ECHOBRAIN
ECONOLINE CRUSH
EDDIE, JOHN
EDISUN
EGYPT CENTRAL
EIGHTEEN VISIONS
ELECTRIC EYE
ELECTRIC LIGHT ORCHESTRA
ELECTRIC REVOLUTION
ELEMENT EIGHTY
EMERGENT
EMISSARY ECHO

EMMICH, VAL
EMMURE
EMPERORS AND ELEPHANTS
EMPHATIC
ENDO
ENTER SHIKARI
EPIDEMIC
EPOXIES, THE
ESCAPE THE FATE
ETHERIDGE, MELISSA
EURYTHMICS
EVANESCENCE
EVANS BLUE
EVERCLEAR
EVERLAST
EVERYDAY LOSERS
EVERY MOTHER'S NIGHTMARE
EVERY TIME I DIE
EVE TO ADAM
EVIL NINE
EVOLOCITY
EXIES, THE
EXODUS
EXTREME
EYE EMPIRE
EYELINERS, THE
FAILURE ANTHEM
FAIR TO MIDLAND
FAITHFULL, MARIANNE
FAITH NO MORE
FAKTION
FALL AS WELL
FALLING REVERSE
FALL OUT BOY
FARRELL, PERRY
FASTBALL

FASTER PUSSYCAT
FATAL KALIBER
FATAL ORDER
FEAR FACTORY
FENIX TX
FEVER 333
FIELDY'S DREAM
FIFTH HARMONY
FIGHT OR FLIGHT
FILTER
FINCH
FINGER 11
FINGERTIGHT
FIREBALL MINISTRY
FIRE FROM THE GODS
FIVE FINGER DEATH PUNCH
FIVE MAN BOLT
FIVE POINTE O
FIVESPEED
FIXX, THE
FLASHPOINT
FLAW
FLECK, BÉLA
FLEETWOOD MAC
FLIPPER
FLO AND EDDIE
FLOGGING MOLLY
FLOOD, THE
FLO RIDA
FLYBANGER
FLYLEAF
FOGERTY, JOHN
FOLKSMEN, THE
FOO FIGHTERS
FORD, LITA
FOREIGNER

FOUNTAINS OF WAYNE
FOUR TOPS, THE
FOXX, JAMIE
FOXY SHAZAM
FRAMPTON, PETER
FRANK CARTER & THE RAT-
TLESNAKES
FRANKIE AND THE KNOCK-
OUTS
FRANKIE GOES TO HOLLY-
WOOD
FREHLEY, ACE
FREY, GLENN
FRIPP, ROBERT
FROM ASHES TO NEW
FROM ZERO
FUEL
FULL DEVIL JACKET
FULL SCALE
FU MANCHU
FUNERAL FOR A FRIEND
FUN LOVIN' CRIMINALS
F-UPS, THE
FUTURE LEADERS OF THE
WORLD
G 3
GABRIEL, PETER
GABRIEL AND THE APOCA-
LYPSE
GALWAY, JAMES
GAMITS, THE
GARBAGE
GARCIA, JERRY
GARY LEWIS & THE PLAYBOYS
G-EAZY
GELDOF, BOB

GEMINI SYNDROME
GENESIS
GFM
GHOST
GHOST HOUNDS
GHOSTS OF AUGUST
GHOULS, THE
GIZMACHI
GLADYS PATCHES
GLASS JAW
GLORIOUS SONS
GO BETTY GO
GODFATHERS, THE
GODFORBID
GODHEAD
GODSMACK
GOGOL BORDELLO
GO GO'S, THE
GOJIRA
GOLDEN EARRING
GOLD MINE SQUAD
GONE BLIND
GOODBARS, THE
GOODBYE JUNE
GOOD CHARLOTTE
GOO GOO DOLLS
GOONS, THE
GORDON, NINA
GOVERNMENT MULE
GRABBITZ
GRADE 8
GRANATI BROTHERS
GRANDE, ARIANA
GRANDMOTHERS, THE
GRANDSON
GRASS ROOTS, THE

GRATEFUL DEAD
GRAVITY KILLS
GRAY, DAVID
GRAYAREA
GREEK FIRE
GREEN DAY
GRETA VAN FLEET
GRISMAN, DAVID
GROBAN, JOSH
GTR
GUIDED BY VOICES
GUNS N' ROSES
GUTTERMOUTH
GUY, BUDDY
H09909
H20
HAGAR, SAMMY
HAIL THE VILLAIN
HAIRBALL
HALESTORM
HALFORD, ROB
HALL AND OATES
HANCOCK, HERBIE
HAND OF THE TRIBE
HANDS LIKE HOUSES
HARMONY RILEY
HARRIS, CALVIN
HARRISON, DHANI
HARRISON, JERRY
HARRY, DEBORAH
HART, MICKEY
HARVEY DANGER
HATEBREED
HAWTHORNE HEIGHTS
HAYES, ISSAC
HAZARD, ROBERT

JAK IT
JANUS
JARS OF CLAY
JEFFREYS, GARLAND
JELLY ROLL
JESSIE J
JETHRO TULL
JETZONS, THE
JETT, JOAN
JIBE
JIMMIE'S CHICKEN SHACK
JOEL, BILLY
JOHANNES, ALAIN
JOHANSEN, DAVID
JOHN, ELTON
JOHN CAFFERTY & THE BEAVER
  BROWN BAND
JOHNSON, JACK
JONES, HOWARD
JONES, TOM
JOURNEY
JOYOUS WOLF
JUDAS PRIEST
JUDD, WYNONNA
JUMP 'N THE SADDLE
KAISER CHIEFS
KAUKONEN, JORMA
KAZ FULLER BAND
KEITH, TOBEY
KENEALLY, MIKE
KESHA
KEYS, ALICIA
KICK
KICKING K8
KICKIN VALENTINA
KID CREOLE & THE COCONUTS

KID ROCK
KIESZA
KILGORE
KILL HANNAH
KILLSWITCH ENGAGE
KING, B. B.
KING, CAROL
KING 810
KING CRIMSON
KINGFISH
KINGSHIFTER
KINKS, THE
KISS
KITTIE
KIX
KLEZMATICS, THE
KONRAD, EVAN
KORN
KOTTONMOUTH KINGS, THE
KRAFTWERK
KRAUSS, ALLISON
KRAVITZ, LENNY
KROKUS
KVELERTAK
KYNG
LA BAMBA & THE HUBCAPS
LABELLE, PATTI
LACUNA COIL
LADY GAGA
LADY LUCK
LAMB OF GOD
LANDES, DAWN
LANDRETH, SONNY
LANEGAN, MARK
LANSDOWNE
LARS FREDERIKSEN AND THE

BASTARDS
LAUPER, CINDY
LAWRENCE ARMS, THE
LEARY, DENIS
LEATHER WOLF
LED ZEPPELIN
LEDFURD, SUNNY
LEE, TOMMY
LEFT ALONE
LEISUREWORLD
LENNOX, ANNIE
LESH, PHIL
LESS THAN JAKE
LETTER KILLS
LET THERE BE SCHOOL OF
ROCK
LEVIN, TONY
LEVINE, ADAM
LIFE OF AGONY
LIFER
LIKE A STORM
LIKE MOTHS TO FLAME
LIL JON
LIMP BIZKIT
LINKIN PARK
LIQUID GANG
LITTLE CAESAR
LITTLE FEAT
LITTLE STEVEN & THE DISCI-
PLES OF SOUL
LIVE
LIVING COLOR
LIVING END, THE
LLOYD, CHER
LLOYD, RICHARD
LOADED

LOCAL H
LOGGINS, KENNY
LOLLIPOP LUST KILL
LONE JUSTICE
LORIN, RACHEL
LOS STRAITJACKETS
LOST PROPHETS
LOU BRUTUS EXPERIENCE,
THE
LOUDERMILK
LOUDNESS
LOUIS XIV
LOVATO, DEMI
LOVE/HATE
LOVE & DEATH
LOVEBLAST
LOWE, NICK
LUNA MORTIS
LYDIA CAN'T BREATHE
LYNAM
LYNNE, JEFF
LYNYRD SKYNYRD
MACHINE GUN KELLY
MACHINE HEAD
MADAM ADAM
MAD AT GRAVITY
MADONNA
MADSIDE
MAE
MAGNA-FI
MAHONE, AUSTIN
MALICE
MANILOW, BARRY
MANMADE GOD
MANN, AIMEE
MANOWAR

MANSON, MARILYN
MAN WITH A MISSION
MARCHING BAND OF THE
  COMBINED SOVIET FORCES IN
  GERMANY
MARLEY, RITA
MARMOZETS
MAROON 5
MARVELOUS 3, THE
MARYANN COTTON
MASEKELA, HUGH
MASTODON
MATCHES, THE
MATREKIS
MATTHEWS, DAVE
MAXIMUM THE HORMONE
MAY, BRIAN
MAYFIELD FOUR
MCCARTNEY, PAUL
MCENTIRE, REBA
MCLACHLAN, SARAH
MDC
MEATLOAF
MEGADETH
MELLENCAMP, JOHN
MELVINS, THE
MEMENTO
MEMPHIS MAY FIRE
MEN AT WORK
MENDES, SHAWN
MENUDO
MERCY FALL
MESHUGGAH
METALLICA
METAL WOLF
METERS, THE

METHADONES, THE
METHENY, PAT
METHODS OF MAYHEM
MIDDLE CLASS RUT
MIDNIGHT OIL
MIDNIGHT TO TWELVE
MIGHTY BLUE KINGS
MIKE AND THE MECHANICS
MILLENCOLIN
MILLER, DENNIS
MILLER, FRANKIE
MILLER, STEVE
MILSAP, RONNIE
MINDLESS SELF INDULGENCE
MINDSET EVOLUTION
MINELLI, LIZA
MINISTRY
MINK DEVILLE
MISSING LETTERS, THE
MISS MAY I
MITCH & MICKEY
MITCHELL, JONI
MOIST
MOLLY HATCHET
MONEY, EDDIE
MONSTER MAGNET
MONSTER TRUCK
MONSTER VOODOO MACHINE
MOORE, IAN
MORELLO, TOM
MORRISON, VAN
MOTHERFEATHER
MOTHER HIPS
MOTIONLESS IN WHITE
MÖTLEY CRÜE
MOTOGRATER

MOTÖRHEAD
MOUNTAIN
MOVEMENTS
MOXY FRÜVOUS
MR. BIG
MUDVAYNE
MUFFIN MEN
MURDERDOLLS
MURPHY, MATT "GUITAR"
MURPHY'S LAW
MUSHROOMHEAD
MUTOID MAN
MXPX
MY CHEMICAL ROMANCE
MY DARKEST DAYS
MY MEMORY REMAINS
MYRRIYA
MY TICKET HOME
N.E.R.D.
NAPALM DEATH
NASH, GRAHAM
NEARLY DEADS, THE
NEBULA
NEIGHBORHOODS, THE
NEKROMANTIX
NELSON
NELSON, WILLIE
NESS, MIKE
NEUROSIS
NEUROSONIC
NEUROTICA
NEVERWAKE
NEVILLE, AARON
NEVILLE BROTHERS, THE
NEW DISEASE
NEW MAIN STREET SINGERS,

THE
NEWMAN, RANDY
NEW MEDICINE
NEW ORDER
NEW RIDERS OF THE PURPLE
SAGE
NEWTON-JOHN, OLIVIA
NEW YEARS DAY
NEW YORK DOLLS
NICKELBACK
NICKS, STEVIE
NIGHTHAWKS, THE
NILE, WILLIE
NINE INCH NAILS
NINE LEFT DEAD
NIRVANA
NIX, RICHIE
NIX, STEVE E.
NIXON, MOJO
NIXONS, THE
NO1CARES
NO ADDRESS
NOFX
NOISE AUCTION
NOISE THERAPY
NONPOINT
NO ONE
NORMA JEAN
NOSE AUCTION
NOTHINGFACE
NOTHING MORE
NO WARNING
NRBQ
NUGENT, TED
NUISANCE
NULLSET

OAK RIDGE BOYS
OASIS
OBLIVIOUS SIGNAL
OCEAN, BILLY
OCTOBER RAGE
OFFSPRING, THE
OF MICE & MEN
OLD VOLTAGE
OLEANDER
ONE LESS REASON
ONE OK ROCK
ONEREPUBLIC
ONESIDEZERO
ONO, YOKO
OPERATOR
OPIATE FOR THE MASSES
OPUS
ORA, RITA
ORANGE 9MM
ORCHESTRAL MANEUVERS IN
  THE DARK
ORGY
ORTON, BETH
OSBOURNE, OZZY
OSMOND, DONNY
OTEP
OTHER ONES, THE
OTHERWISE
OUR DAUGHTER'S WEDDING
OUR LADY PEACE
OUTFIELD, THE
OUTHOUSE
OUTLAWS, THE
OVERWHELMING COLORFAST
O'BROTHER
O'CONNOR, SINEAD

P.I.L.
P.O.D.
PACIFIER
PAGE AND PLANT
PALAYE ROYALE
PALISADES
PANTERA
PAPA ROACH
PARAMORE
PARKER, GRAHAM
PARKWAY DRIVE
PARLIAMENT/FUNKADELIC
PARSONS, ALAN
PAUL, HENRY
PAUL, LES
PEARL JAM
PENN, MICHEAL
PENN AND TELLER
PENNYWISE
PEPPER
PERIPHERY
PERRI, CHRISTINA
PETTY, TOM
PHENOMENAUTS, THE
PHISH
PHOSPHENE
PHOTEK
PICARD
PIERCE THE VEIL
PIETASTERS, THE
PILLAR
PIMPADELIC
PINK FLOYD
PIPER
PIRANHA
PITCHSHIFTER

PIXIES, THE
PLACEBO
PLANT, ROBERT
POINDEXTER, BUSTER
POISON
POLLACK, NEAL
POP, IGGY
POP EVIL
PORCUPINE TREE
POWERMAN 5000
POWER STATION
POWER TRIP
PRANKSTER, MARY
PRAY FOR SLEEP
PRESIDENTS OF THE UNITED
 STATES OF AMERICA, THE
PRESTON, BILLY
PRETENDERS, THE
PRETTY RECKLESS, THE
PRIMER 55
PRIMUS
PROJECT 86
PROM KINGS
PRONG
PROPHETS OF ADDICTION
PROPHETS OF RAGE
PSY
PSYCHEDELIC FURS
PSYCHOTICA
PT 109
PUBLIC ENEMY
PUDDLE OF MUDD
PUENTE, TITO
PULSE ULTRA
PURE RUBBISH
PUSH MONKEY

PUSSY RIOT
PUYA
QUARTERFLASH
QUEEN
QUEENS OF THE STONE AGE
QUEENSRŸCHE
QUEERS, THE
QUICKSAND
QUIGLEY, JACK (AND HIS ONLY
 FRIEND)
R.E.M.
RA
RADATTACK
RADKEY
RAGE AGAINST THE MACHINE
RAINBOW
RAIN DOGS, THE
RAITT, BONNIE
RAMMSTEIN
RAMONES, THE
RANCID
RASPBERRIES, THE
RATDOG
RATTLEHEAD
RAYE BAND, BENJAMIN
REACHAROUND
REAL KNIVES
RED
REDBONE, LEON
RED FANG
RED HOT CHILI PEPPERS
RED JUMPSUIT APPARATUS
REDLIGHT KING
RED LINE CHEMISTRY
RED RIDER
RED SUN RISING

REED, LOU
REEL BIG FISH
REFUSED
REID SPEED
REO SPEEDWAGON
REPLACEMENTS, THE
RESIDENTS, THE
REVEILLE
REVENANT SOUL
REVEREND HORTON HEAT
REVOLUTION SMILE, THE
REV THEORY
REXA, BEBE
RICH, BUDDY
RICHARDS, KEITH
RIDDLIN' KIDS
RISE AGAINST
RIVAL SONS
RIVERBOAT GAMBLERS
ROADRUNNER UNITED
ROCKET FROM THE CRYPT
ROCKETS, THE
ROCKPILE
ROLLING BLACKOUTS, THE
ROLLING STONES
ROLLINS, HENRY
ROLLINS BAND
ROMANTICS, THE
RONSON, MICK
ROOMFUL OF BLUES
ROSSINGTON BAND
ROTH, DAVID LEE
ROXZ
ROYAL BLISS
ROYAL REPUBLIC
RUMOURS, THE

RUNDGREN, TODD
RUN DMC
RUSH
RUTLES, THE
SABATRON
SAIGON KICK
SAINT ASONIA
SALIVA
SANFORD-TOWNSEND BAND
SANTA CRUZ
SANTANA
SAOSIN
SATYRICON
SAVATAGE
SAVE FERRIS
SAVING ABEL
SAXON
SCAGGS, BOZ
SCALLIONS, BRETT
SCARLET CANARY
SCARLXRD
SCARS ON BROADWAY
SCARY KIDS SCARING KIDS
SCATTERED HAMLET
SCHON, NEIL
SCORPION CHILD
SCORPIONS, THE
SCOTCH GREENS, THE
SCREAMING FOR SILENCE
SCREAMING TREES
SEAL
SEASONS AFTER
SEEGER, BOB
SEETHER
SEMISONIC
SENSES FAIL

SEPARATE CHECKS
SEPTEMBER MOURNING
SEPULTURA
SETZER, BRIAN
SEV
SEVEN DAY SONNET
SEVENDUST
SEVEN MARY THREE
SHADOWS FALL
SHALLOW SIDE
SHAMAN'S HARVEST
SHEERAN, ED
SHEPARD, KENNY WAYNE
SHIM
SHINDELL, RICHARD
SHINEDOWN
SHOOTING GALLERY
SHRAPNEL
SHRINE, THE
SHUVEL
SHVPES
SICK F*CKS, THE
SICK PUPPIES
SILENCE IS BROKEN
SILENCE THE MIND
SILVERCHAIR
SILVERGUN
SILVER SNAKES
SILVERSYDE
SILVERTUNG
SIMON, PAUL
SIMON & GARFUNKEL
SIMON SAYS
SIN 7
SINATRA, FRANK
SINCE OCTOBER

SINCH
SIN CITY ESCAPE
SINNISSTAR
SINOMATIC
SKID ROW
SKILLET
SKINDRED
SKRAPE
SLASH
SLASHTONES, THE
SLAUGHTER
SLAVES ON DOPE
SLAYER
SLEEPING WITH SIRENS
SLIPKNOT
SLITHERYN
SLO BURN
SLOTH
SMASHING PUMPKINS, THE
SMASHMOUTH
SMILE EMPTY SOUL
SMILING POLITELY
SMITH, WILL
SMITHEREENS, THE
SMOKE OR FIRE
SNAKE RIVER CONSPIRACY
SNIDER, DEE
SNOOP DOGG
SNOT
SOAK
SOCIAL BURN
SOCIAL DISTORTION
SOIL
SOILWORK
SONICVOID
SONIC YOUTH

SOUL ASYLUM
SOUL COUGHING
SOULFLY
SOULWAX
SOUNDGARDEN
SOUTHERN CULTURE ON THE
  SKIDS
SOUTHERN GOVERNOR
SOUTHSIDE JOHNNY AND THE
  ASBURY JUKES
SOVIETTES, THE
SPARTA
SPEAK NO EVIL
SPECIALS, THE
SPINAL TAP
SPINESHANK
SPIRACELL
SPIRIT ANIMAL
SPONGE
SPRINGFIELD, RICK
SPRINGSTEEN, BRUCE
SQUEEZE
SQUIER, BILLY
STABBING WESTWARD
STAIND
STANDING ALLIANCE
STANLEY, PAUL
STAPLETON, CHRIS
STAPP, SCOTT
STARE ACROSS
STARR, RINGO
STARSET
STARS IN STEREO
STATE YOUR CAUSE
STATIC X
STATION

STEEL PANTHER
STEELY DAN
STEPPENWOLF
STEREOMUD
STEREOPHONICS
STEWART, ROD
STILLS, STEPHEN
STILLWATER
STING
STING
STIR
STITCHED UP HEART
STONE, SLY
STONE SOUR
STONE TEMPLE PILOTS
STORMBREAKER
STORY OF THE YEAR
STORY SO FAR, THE
STRANGE DAZE
STRATA
STRATA
STRATE
STRAY CATS, THE
STREET DRUM CORPS
STREETLIGHT CIRCUS
STRETCH ARMSTRONG
STRUNG OUT
STRUTS, THE
STRYPER
STUN
STURM, LACEY
STYX
SUBMERSED
SUGARCUBES
SUGAR RAY
SUICIDAL TENDENCIES

SUICIDE SILENCE

SUM 41

SUNFLOWER DEAD

SUNSET BLACK

SUPERJOINT RITUAL

SUPERSUCKERS

SURRENDER THE FALL

SWIFT, TAYLOR

SWINGIN' MEDALLIONS, THE

SWITCHED

SWORD, THE

SWORN ENEMY

SYDONIA

SYLAR

SYSTEMATIC

SYSTEM OF A DOWN

TADDY PORTER

TAKING BACK SUNDAY

TAKING DAWN

TALENT, BILLY

TANGIER

TANKIAN, SERJ

TANTRIC

TAPROOT

TAYLOR, JAMES

TEAM CYBERGEIST

TEARS FOR FEARS

TECH N9NE

TEENAGE WRIST

TEMPLE OF THE DOG

TEN FOOT POLE

TESLA

TESTAMENT

TEXAS HIPPIE COALITION

THEM EVILS

THEO & THE SKYSCRAPERS

THEORY OF A DEADMAN

THEY MIGHT BE GIANTS

THIRD KIND

THIRD STRIKE

THIRTY SECONDS TO MARS

THOMAS, IRMA

THOMAS, ROB

THOMPSON, HUNTER S.

THOMPSON TWINS, THE

THORNLEY

THOROGOOD, GEORGE

THOSE DARN ACCORDIONS

THOUSAND FOOT KRUTCH

THREE DAYS GRACE

THRICE

THROUGH FIRE

THROWDOWN

THUNDERS, JOHNNY

TIGER ARMY

TIL TUESDAY

TIME AGAIN

TIN MACHINE

TOADIES

TOMAHAWK

TOM TOM CLUB

TONIC

TOOL

TOOTHGRINDER

TOUSSAINT, ALLEN

TOWNSHEND, PETE

TRAGICALLY HIP, THE

TRAINOR, MEGHAN

TRANSPLANTS, THE

TRAPT

TREMONTI

TRIVIUM

TRIXTER

TROUT FISHING IN AMERICA

TROWER, ROBIN

TRUCKFIGHTERS

TRUST COMPANY

TRUTH FOR TREASON

T.T. QUICK

TUBES, THE

TURNER, TINA

TURNSTILE

TURTLES, THE

TWELVE FOOT NINJA

TWIN CAM

TWISTED METHOD

TWISTED SISTER

TWIZTID

TWO SKINNEE J'S

**TYLER BRYANT & THE SHAKE-
DOWN**

TYPE O NEGATIVE

U.K.

U2

UB40

UGLY KID JOE

ULTRASPANK

UNCLE FLOYD SHOW, THE

UNDEROATH

UNEARTH

UNION UNDERGROUND

UNLOCKING THE TRUTH

UNLOCO

UNWRITTEN LAW

UPON A BURNING BODY

USED, THE

UTOPIA

VAI, STEVE

VALIENT THORR

VALLEJO

VALORA

VANDALS, THE

VAN HALEN

VAUDEVILLE

VAUGHN, STEVIE RAY

VAUX

VEDDER, EDDIE

VEER UNION, THE

VEIL OF MAYA

VEILSIDE

VELVET REVOLVER

VENTURES, THE

VERSUS ME

VERUCA SALT

VERVE PIPE, THE

VIA

VIDEODRONE

VIMIC

VINNIE VINCENT INVASION

VIOLENT FEMMES

VIOLENT SOHO

VISION OF DISORDER

VIXEN

VOIVOD

VOLBEAT

WAGE WAR

WAINWRIGHT, VICTOR

WAITS, TOM

WAKEMAN, RICK

WALDOS, THE

WALKER, BUTCH

WALKER, JOE LOUIS

WALLS OF JERICHO

WALSH, JOE

WANDERLUST

WARRANT

WASHINGTON SOCIAL CLUB

WATERS, ROGER

WATERSHED

WATT, ANDREW

WAYLAND

WE ARE HARLOT

WE AS HUMAN

WE CAME AS ROMANS

WEDNESDAY 13

WEEZER

WEILAND, SCOTT

WEIR, BOB

WEIR, BOB AND WOLF BROTH-
ERS

WELCH, BOB

WERM

WEST, KANYE

WHILE SHE SLEEPS

WHISTLER, PAUL

WHITECHAPEL

WHITE ZOMBIE

WHO, THE

WHOLE WHEAT BREAD

WICKED WISDOM

WILDER, WEBB

WILD THRONE

WILLIAMS JR., HANK

WILSON

WILSON, BRIAN

WILSON, RITA

WINGER

WINWOOD, STEVE

WOLF, PETER

WOLFMOTHER

WONDER, STEVIE

WRECKED

WYLDE, ZAKK

WYNONNA

XCX, CHARLI

X FACTOR ONE

XTC

YANKOVIC, "WEIRD AL"

YEAR LONG DISASTER

YEAR OF THE LOCUST

YELAWOLF

YES

YOU ME AT SIX

YOUNG, NEIL

YOUNG, PAUL

YOUNG GUNS

YUMM, VAL

YUNGBLUD

YUPPIE PRICKS, THE

ZAKK SABBATH

ZAPPA, FRANK

ZEAL & ARDOR

ZEALOTS, THE

ZEVON, WARREN

ZOMBIE, ROB

ZZ TOP